Published by Web Publishing

This anthology copyright © 2016 Aubrey Malone

Aubrey Malone has asserted his
right under the Copyright, Designs and Patents Act
1988 to be identified as the editor of this work.

ISBN 978-1-53992-769-3

Also available as a Kindle ebook
ISBN 978-1-84396-431-5

A catalogue record for this
book is available from the British Library
and the American Library of Congress

Pre-press production
eBook Versions
27 Old Gloucester Street
London WC1N 3AX
www.ebookversions.com

SHOOTING
FROM
THE LIP

AN ANTHOLOGY OF
MUSICAL INVECTIVE AND WIT

Edited by Aubrey Malone

WEB PUBLISHING

Contents

I'd Hate To Be You

Boy George is all England needs - another queen who can't dress.
Joan Rivers

This guy rattles up the concrete stairs. He's almost vibrating, like he got his fingers stuck in an electric socket. Twitch central. He looks like a hobo who struck oil and then plumb forgot where the durn well was. His eyes are like two foxes frantically searching for a hole to hide in. This guy: He'd get bruised by a shadow.
B.P.Fallon on seeing Bob Dylan in Dublin in 1966

Madonna shaved her legs to lose thirty pounds.
Joan Rivers

Bob Geldof may have saved some lives in Africa with 'Do They Know It's Christmas' but nobody talks about the torture the song inflicted on the British public.
Morrissey

That half-melted vanilla face.
Brad Darrack on Elvis Presley

With the sales of his new single collapsing, Ronan Keating has been revealing fascinating insights about his life. He's being stalked. He'd rather be poor than give up sex. He likes Jack Daniels. If only pop's Mr Clean would add that he's also a rubbish singer.
Mary Carr

A nobody who needed a somebody to be anybody.
Constant Meijers on Elvis Presley's manager, Tom Parker

Morrissey sometimes brings out records with the greatest titles in the world. Which, somewhere along the line, he neglects to write songs for.
Elvis Costello

Leonard, we know you're great. We just don't know if you're any good.
Columbia Records president Walter Yetnikoff to Leonard Cohen in 1984

Pop stars usually have the intelligence quotient of a piece of toast.
Joseph O'Connor

The problem with Lloyd Webber's music isn't that it sounds as if it was written by somebody else. The problem is that it sounds like it was written by Lloyd Webber.
Gerald Kaufman

For most rockers, the only thing standing between them and total illiteracy is the need to get through their Mercedes-Benz owner's manual.
Garry Trudeau

I like Don Rickles but that's because I have no taste.
Frank Sinatra

Liberace reeks of emetic language that can make grown men long for a quiet corner, a handkerchief and an aspidistra. Without doubt he is the biggest sentimental vomit of all time.
Daily Mail

I had a dream the other night about music critics. They were small and rodent-like, with padlock ears. They looked like they'd stepped out of a painting by Goya.
Igor Stravinsky

The gigs I enjoy most are the ones where I hate the audience.
Shane MacGowan

Even stupid people in Britain are smarter than Americans.
Madonna

Folk music is just a bunch of fat people.
Bob Dylan

Maurice Chevalier is a sort of male duenna with a leer-face lifted into a smile.
David Thompson

I despise the royalty. I've never met anyone who supports them except some deaf elderly pensioner in Hartlepool who has pictures of Prince Edward pinned on the toilet seat.
Morrissey

Your hair is a mess. You talk with a plum in your mouth and your trousers come up to your neck.
Failed Pop Idol contestant to Simon Cowell

I don't trust people whose last names sound like first names.
Jay McInerney on George Michael

Marlene Dietrich is devoid of graciousness. She's rude to everyone. She's hard of hearing. She's got an old lady's stoop. She insults nearly everyone who gets near her. She's a complainer. She's impossible to satisfy. She behaves like an idiot and gets more mileage on less talent than anyone I know. But apart from that I like her.
Earl Wilson

An ill-conceived nostalgia award wrenched from the rancid prostates of senile, gibbering hippies.
Irvine Welsh's reaction to Bob Dylan being awarded the Nobel Prize for Literature in 2016

Sinead O'Connor has the sex appeal of a Venetian blind.
Madonna

JOKERMAN

Cats closed today after 18 years. Any cast members not adopted after four weeks will be put to sleep.
Jay Leno

What's the difference between a soprano and a pit bull? The jewellery, darling, the jewellery.
Carlo May

How did we find America? We turned left at Greenland.
Ringo Starr

What's the difference between the James Last orchestra and a bull? A bull has the horns at the front and the arsehole at the back.
Damien Corless

Why did Ronan Keating cross the road? To get to the middle.
Patrick Taylor

What's Sammy Davis' favourite TV show? *Popeye*!
Red Buttons

How does Ozzy Osbourne change a lightbulb? He bites off the old one.
Carlo May

Do you know why Michael Jackson called one of his albums 'Bad'? Because he couldn't spell 'Pathetic.'
Prince

What's black and screams? Stevie Wonder answering the iron.
Joe Morrison

Why do I wear all these ring on my fingers? Because I can't get them all through my nose.
Ringo Starr

What do you call a dog with wings? Linda McCartney.
Michael Harkness

I'm not saying Pavarotti was fat but his bum began around his neck.
Jasper Carrott

What did the guitarist do when he was told to turn on his amp? He told it that he loved it.
Carlo May

I bumped into Dolly Parton the other day. What made it unusual was that I was on the other side of the street at the time.
Bob Monkhouse

What's eighteen inches long and hangs in front of an asshole? Daniel O'Donnell's tie.
Norman Bowles

How many country and western singers does it take to change a lightbulb? Seven. One to put in the new bulb and six to sing a song about how good the old one was.
Ben Forest

Why are there so many violinists in an orchestra? Because the conductor actually wants someone to play the right note.
Bruno Kassel

What goes 'Me me me me me'? Victoria Beckham practising the octave. Or talking about life's priorities.
Desmond Grealish

How many drummers does it take to wallpaper a room? Three if you slice them thinly enough.
Tommy Cooper

Paul McCartney once bought Heather a plane for her birthday. She used Immac for the other leg.
Steve Ferris

My ambition is to become senile.
Prince

With the collapse of vaudeville, new talent has no place to stink any more.
George Burns

Have you heard about the Scotsman who left his bagpipes in the back seat of his car with the windows open? When he got back, there was another set beside them.
E.K. Kruger

The world's greatest optimist is a banjo player with a pager.
Fred Metcalf

What did Cher say the first time she made love? 'I didn't know all you guys were on the same team.'
Johnny Carson

Did you hear about the concert pianist who was working on a new arrangement? It then turned out his wife wasn't away for the weekend after all.
Jackie Mason

The reason Dolly Parton's feet are so small is because things don't grow well in the shade.
Joan Rivers

Mariah Carey made it to the top because her dresses didn't.
Don Rickles

Jennifer Lopez slept her way to the middle.
Bob Oritz

Latest news bulletin from Memphis: Elvis is Still Dead.
Mort Sahl

I hear Dolly Parton is writing her autobiography. She's calling it *Twin Peaks*.
Bret Hogarth

Tribute acts have been all the go for a few years. Apparently there's a band doing the rounds in Glasgow that's modelled on the former chart-topping boyband Take That. It's called 'Take That, Ya Bastart'.
Michael Munro

Last night Sammy Davis asked me what I'd like to drink to. I replied, 'To about four in the morning.'
Dean Martin

I believe Cher and Madonna have fallen out. They're not on first name terms anymore.
Jo Brand

They've named a new soup after Daniel O'Donnell. Thick Country Vegetable.
Gene Fitzpatrick

Do you think Rod Stewart is sexy? I'm not even sure he's even alive.
Barbara Ellen

Winning the Eurovision once might be deemed unfortunate. Winning it twice is carelessness. Three times and you'd better quit while you're behind.
Declan Lynch on the success of Johnny Logan in the event

A Russian String Trio is a Russian String Quartet that came back from the West.
David Steel

What's the difference between Walt Disney and Frank Sinatra? One sings and the other disnae.
Tommy McTaig

When the Beatles first arrived in America they were 40 pounds overweight. And that was just their hair.
Bob Hope

Taylor Swift met a guy a strange way the other day. They were introduced.
Michael Harkness

Why can't you be a Boyzone fan if you've been circumcised? Because you have to be a complete prick to be a Boyzone fan.
Dessie Ferguson

I've been listening to a sonata written by Chopin in A flat. You'd think with the sort of money he was earning he'd be able to afford a house.
Alastair McGowan

I once drove into a garage where Anthony Newley was the petrol pump. He was singing 'What Kind of Fuel Am I?'
Eric Morecambe

The whole point of entering the Eurovision Song Contest is to try to come last, a coveted position which the crafty Finns have more or less cornered for years before the Irish usurped it.
Karl Shaw

I could eat alphabet soup and shit better lyrics than he does.
Johnny Mercer on an acquaintance

A fugue is a piece of music in which the voices come in one after the other. And the audience go out one after the other.
Sydney Wahlberg

What has a hundred legs and no teeth? The front row of a Daniel O'Donnell concert.
Jimmy MacCormack

What has 180 legs and no pubic hair? The front row of a Justin Bieber concert.
Mike Hamilton

Dudley Moore is such a clever little pianist. He can play on the white keys as well as the black ones.
Noel Coward

The Detroit String Quartet played Brahms last night. Brahms lost.
Bennett Cerf

The other day I phoned my local pizza delivery firm and asked for a thin crusty supreme. They sent me Diana Ross.
Henny Youngman

I hate music, especially when it's played.
Jimmy Durante

Stevie Wonder's favourite book was *Around the Block in 80 Days*.
Phelim Hughes

I believe scientists have found a new solar system. There are one or two stars surrounded by three darkish lumps. Would that not be Boyzone?
Frank Skinner

She's got a promising voice. Here's hoping she promises not to take up singing as a career.
George Burns

I heard Elvis Presley was an autosexual. Did that mean he loved himself or cars?
Keenan Wynn

We're told Barry Manilow is one of America's best contributions to world culture. You're talking about a guy whose main fanbase is overweight Catholic teenagers.
Denis Leary

Sinead O'Connor has a walk-in wardrobe. And a walk-in mouth.
Frank Sinatra

What's yellow and lives off beetles? Yoko Ono.
Joe Morrison

If Dire Straits joined up with Chris Rea, they could call themselves Diarrhoea.
Eanna Brophy

What would you call 2,000 banjos thrown into the river Clyde? A good start.
Tom Shields

I'm writing Kylie Minogue's biography. I'm going to call it *Superstar, Jesus Christ!*
Barry Cryer

I'd like you to play us a medley of your hit.
Oscar Levant to George Gershwin

How did Michael Jackson pick his nose? From a catalogue.
Rod Sterling

A quartet is a singing group in which all four think the other three can't sing.
Bryan Lyden

People ask why Cliff Richard is still the Bachelor Boy. Wrong - he's married to himself. Every night when he goes home he throws his arms around himself and tells himself how much he loves him.
Scott Bryant

Whenever I get a bad review I cry my way to the bank.
Liberace

People tell me I'm indecisive. Personally, I'm not so sure.
Sandie Shaw

A folk singer is someone who sings through his nose by ear.
Arnold Powell

Wagner's music is better than it sounds.
Mark Twain

I love Beethoven, especially his poems.
Ringo Starr

I've never heard any Stockhausen but I do believe I have stepped
in some from time to time.
Sir Thomas Beecham

What would you call a tennis match between Stevie Wonder
and Helen Keller? Endless love.
Denis Leary

Michael Jackson was a man of many parts.
Arnold Bailey

Tenors get women by the score.
James Joyce

That's quite a dress Beyonce is almost wearing.
David Letterman)

Subterranean Homesick Blues

I went to a blues bar last night but the singer was in a good mood so she cancelled the show.
Debbie Kasper

Celine Dion went into a bar to get a drink. The barman said, 'Why the long face?'
Joan Carswell

Blues music is about having nothing and then losing it. It's like, 'I don't even have a guitar. I'm strumming my bellybutton.'
Dylan Moran

Why are blues songs so simple? So blues singers can understand them.
Paul Morrison

You know the song 'Broken Alarm Clock Blues'? It's the one that begins, 'Woke up this afternoon.'
Steven Wright

In blues music, 'Adulthood' means being old enough to get the electric chair if you shoot a man in Memphis.
Paul Cloutman

I love Van Morrison's music. It's a pity he's such a miserable bugger.
Rod Stewart

Leonard Cohen's records should be sold with razor blades.
Michael Harkness

I had a nightmare that I was trapped in an elevator with Geri Halliwell and Bryan MacFadden and I had only one bullet in my gun.
Mark Lamarr

The best epitaph for a blues singer would be, '*Didn't* wake up this morning.'
Burl Ives

The last telegram from the Titanic was recently auctioned off. It said, 'Help! They won't stop playing that Celine Dion song.' And then everyone killed themselves.
Conan O'Brien

See That My
Grave is Kept Clean

All my heroes are dead. Keith Richards for instance.
Bill Hicks

Elvis died sitting on the lavvy. When you gotta go you gotta go.
Jackie Mason

Old session musicians never die. They just fake away.
Steve Ellis

Shakespeare had a sad life. After all, he didn't live long enough
to collaborate with Andrew Lloyd Webber.
Victoria Wood

Jimi Hendrix died in a pool of his own vomit. Do you know
how much you have to puke to fill a pool?
Bill Hicks

The only good thing about the eighties was that we got rid of
one of the Bee Gees. One down, three to go.
Denis Leary

The first requirement of a composer is that he be dead.
Arthur Honegger

Do you remember where you were when Elvis died? I was pulling the pins out of my Elvis doll.
Doug Benson

Jimi Hendrix, deceased, drugs. Janis Joplin, deceased, alcohol. Mama Cass, deceased, ham sandwich.
Mike Myers

It's All Over Now, Baby Blue

The bad news is that Boyzone don't like us anymore. The good news is that they're all moving to England.
Brendan O'Connor

The other day Britney Spears was spotted leaving a club with her new boyfriend. As they were driving away, she vomited on the guy. Music experts are calling it her best release in years.
Conan O'Brien

Billy Joel is so derivative, he even ripped off his motorcycle accident from Bob Dylan.
Jon Stewart

My attempt to get rid of mice proved futile so I played Cat Stevens records. Sadly, that was no good either. It seems to work on humans but not rodents.
Jacqueline Kavanagh

Gareth Gates: the pop equivalent of aquarium gravel.
Mark Lamarr

I don't know anyone who's made a decent record in the last twenty years.
Bob Dylan

There's a pecking order for celebrities at after-show parties. One time both Prince and Madonna circled a block in their limos for twenty minutes because neither of them wanted to be the first to arrive.
Graham Norton

Dave Gahan of Depeche Mode has a pierced perineum, which is the bit between the scrotum and the arsehole. Just think Sharon Osbourne in between Simon Cowell and Louis Walsh.
Mark Lamarr

Nobody dates the drummer.
Gene Krupa

Drew Barrymore sings so badly, deaf people refuse to watch her lips move.
Woody Allen

When Danni Minogue was a child, a dingo ran off with her talent.
Mark Lamarr

You have to admire Madonna. She hides her lack of talent so well.
Manolo Blahnik

Harpists spend 90% of their lives tuning their harps and the other 10% playing out of tune.
Igor Stravinsky

The Finnish band that won Eurovision in 2006 had all the sophistication of an AC/DC tribute band, and a wardrobe borrowed from the extras in one of the less believable episodes of *Xena, Warrior Princess.*
Brendan O'Connor

When the batteries run down on my Walkman Bob Dylan still sounds the same.
Lance Crowther

Peter Andre: the most unwelcome comeback since Jimi Hendrix' vomit.
Mark Lamarr

Let's be easy on Eminem. At the end of the day he's just another white guy trying to make an honest living stealing black people's music.
Comic Dog

Celine Dion was in a 4000-seat auditorium built specially to handle her voice but it didn't work. I could still hear her.
Lewis Black

Michael Bolton had nine hits this year. On his website.
Dame Edna Everage

In Kafka's book *Metamorphosis* the protagonist wakes up one day believing himself to be a beetle. Do you think Noel Gallagher suffers from this?

Jimmy Carr

My Back Pages

I lost my virginity as a career move.
Madonna

In the third grade a nun stuffed me in a garbage can under her desk because she said that's where I belonged.
Bruce Springsteen

I was never molested as a child. Unfortunately.
Elton John

From when I was very young I just knew that being a girl and being charming in a feminine sort of way could get me a lot of things. I milked it for everything I could.
Madonna

I was ignored by the universe as a child. I spent my whole childhood with my head buried in a pillow.
Morrissey

When my mother died, I made a conscious decision to smoke myself to death.
Sinead O'Connor

I went to school in a place where they tell you to wed a dentist.
Barbra Streisand

In High School I took an aptitude test. It said I was 98% guaranteed to be a mechanic.
K.D. Lang

I was born at the age of 12 on the MGM lot.
Judy Garland

Dad said I had a voice like a coalman.
Lulu

I was mad on the Dubliners as a kid – especially the dirty songs.
Shane MacGowan

Shortly after we formed The Boomtown Rats I set fire to my father's house.
Bob Geldof

I got into music because my nose was so big I couldn't get any girls.
Pete Townshend

When I was a little kid I wanted to be an old man. I wanted a limp and a hat and a cane and a coat and a beard. Nowadays I feel a lot younger so I'm kinda living upside down.
Tom Waits

My childhood is so far away it's like it happened to someone else.
Bob Dylan

I was born in a crossfire hurricane.
Mick Jagger

My first gig was like being dead with none of the benefits.
Barry Manilow

When I was growing up, there were two things that were unpopular in my house. One was me and the other was my guitar.
Bruce Springsteen

My mother only wanted me to get good grades at school so she could brag to the other women in the bridge club.
Jim Morrison

I never had an adolescence. I went straight from 6 to 46.
Morrissey

My first memory is of raping the babysitter. She was 15 and I was 5.
Eminem

Is Your Love in Vain?

I was in love once and it was an awful experience. It rotted me. It was a disease.
David Bowie

People used to hate me and now they love me. Not that I give a damn either way.
Cher

It's possible to go through life without loving or being loved.
Morrissey

A May–December wedding is one thing, but BC–AD?
Jim Mullen on the romance between Barbra Streisand and Andre Agassi

Whenever you're feeling cheap and nasty, remind yourself that without infidelity, literature and music would be up shit creek.
Kathy Lette

If music be the food of love, why do The Eurythmics insist on

serving up spam and chips all the time?
Pauline McGurk

We have a love-hate relationship. He loves me and I hate him.
Jeff Beck on Rod Stewart

The only kind of friendship Brian Jones could tolerate was unconditional love.
Marianne Faithfull

The hippies wanted peace and love but we wanted Ferraris, blondes and switchblades.
Alice Cooper

Yes, no, yes, no, yes, no.
Morrissey after being asked if he ever fell in love

Love isn't the dying moan of a distant violin. It's the triumphant twang of a bedspring.
S.J. Perelman

Tonight I'll Be
Staying Here With You

I saw a sign outside McDonalds the other day: 'Over 13 Billion Served.' Would that not be Madonna?
Clive Barry

Jordan went out with Gareth Gates, which is the dictionary definition of tit for tat.
Mark Lamarr

I'm aroused by the idea of a woman making love to me while either a man or another woman watches.
Madonna

Most people get into bands for three very simple reasons. To get rich, to get famous and to get laid.
Bob Geldof

I'm the only man who can say he's been in Take That and at least two members of The Spice Girls.
Robbie Williams

Rod Stewart is a man of principle. He will not go out with a woman with brown hair.
David Walliams

The main difference between Michael Jackson and Bill Clinton is that Jackson tried to convince us he *did* have sex with women.
David Letterman

David used sex the way a cat sprays, to mark his territory.
Angela Bowie

It would be great to be both sexes.
Madonna

Most queens would like nothing more than to live out their fantasies with a member of the armed forces. We all love a man in uniform.
Boy George

The world doesn't revolve around the sun, it revolves around a giant cock.
Marilyn Manson

I'm a John Denver freak. I don't give a shit that he looks like a fucking turkey.
Grace Slick

I love Dolly Parton. I don't know why. Maybe it's a subconscious desire to breastfeed.
Graham Norton

It's not easy being in a group. It's like marriage without sex.
Sting

I knew it was time to stop cheating when I was with my girlfriend and I found myself fantasising about my wife.
Mick Jagger

Seeing the
Real You At Last

Bob Dylan is a sophisticated con man pretending to be a sentimental hillbilly.
Truman Capote

Elgar is one of the Seven Humbugs of Christendom.
George Bernard Shaw

When my enemies stop hissing, I know I'm slipping.
Maria Callas

By the end of his life, Elvis had turned into an Elvis impersonator.
Tara McAdams

Am I happy Ronan Keating hasn't done well? Of course.
Louis Walsh

Rolf Harris is a difficult man to hate but that doesn't mean we shouldn't try.
A.A. Gill

A deadly winking, sniggering, snuggling, chromium-plated, scent-impregnated, luminous, quivering, giggling, mincing heap of mother love.
William Connor on Liberace

A skinny, no-talent, stupid Hoboken bastard.
Shelley Winters on Frank Sinatra

Kylie Minogue was very clever in the video *Spinning Around*. She realised that her voice was not the most important part of her career but rather her bum.
Simon Cowell

Frankie Laine's approach to the microphone is that of an accused man pleading with a hostile jury.
Kenneth Tynan

The Beatles are dying in the wrong order.
Victor Lewis-Smith

Licence to Kill

Being noticed can be a burden. Jesus was crucified because he got himself noticed. So I disappear a lot.
Bob Dylan

Support the arts. Kill a drummer.
Bumper Sticker

Let me make sure I'm clear on this issue. Heavy metal fans are buying heavy metal records, taking them home, listening to them and then blowing their heads off with shotguns. So where's the problem?
Denis Leary

If I feel like killing a hippie, I will. I don't have to be angry to do that. I'm more of a robot than a person.
Sid Vicious

A few years ago, Daniel O'Donnell's manager insisted he be shifted to the middle-of-the-road charts. It wasn't the middle of the road during rush hour, unfortunately.
Seconds Out

Why did Beethoven kill all his chickens? Because they kept going around the place saying 'Bach! Bach! Bach!'
Bob Monkhouse

My attitude to men who mess around is simple: If you find 'em, kill 'em.
Loretta Lynn

You know how sometimes you have a song going through your head over and over all day long and it's driving you crazy because you can't get it out of your mind? Well I know how to fix that. It's extreme but it works every time. You kill yourself.
George Carlin

If there's to be a chair for critics let it be an electric one.
Sir Thomas Beecham

Music hath charm to sooth a savage beast but I'd try a revolver first.
Josh Billings

The man has to die. The sonofabitch must go. There's too much pain in me and he caused it. You will do it for me. Kill the sonofabitch, Sonny.
Elvis Presley to his bodyguard Sonny West about Mike Stone after he learned Stone had slept with his wife

The next time she crosses a street I hope four blind guys come along driving trucks.
Frank Sinatra on his biographer Kitty Kelley

If Prince came from Wigan he would have been slaughtered the second he stepped on a stage.
Morrissey

The only way we're going to have a Beatles reunion now is if we shoot the other two.
Denis Leary

Why did Mark Chapman shoot John Lennon? Yoko ducked.
Lucille Oritz

Anita Bryant tells us she's afraid of being assassinated. She needn't worry. The only people who would be interested in killing her are music-lovers.
Gore Vidal

If I met someone like myself I'd probably kill them.
Madonna

When I met Jerry Lee Lewis I went in there quaking. He offered me some whiskey. He said 'You either drink with me or I shoot you.' So I drank with him.
Shane MacGowan

The best way to get two viola players to play in unison is to shoot one of them.
Mike Haskins

The other day I was sitting around the house listening to some Alanis Morrisette when the doorbell rang. So I slipped the gun out of my mouth.
Vernon Chatman

Tchaikovsky thought of committing suicide for fear of being discovered as a homosexual. Today if you're a composer and *not* homosexual, you might as well put a bullet through your head.
Sergei Diaghilev

If I had an axe I'd kill everyone except my friends.
Jim Morrison

Blowin' in the Wind

An oboe is an ill wind that nobody can blow good.
Bennett Cerf

Never look at trombonists. It only encourages them.
Richard Strauss

The bagpipes are instruments of torture consisting of a leaky bag and punctured pipes, played by blowing up the bag and placing your fingers over the wrong holes.
Dick Diabolus

Bob Dylan didn't burn the candle at both ends. He used a blowtorch in the middle instead.
Richard Farina

How can you tell if a bagpipe is out of tune? Someone is blowing into it.
Bernard Manning

Bagpipes rise and fall like a weight swung in the air at the end of a string.
Hugh MacDiarmid

Are you producing as much sound as possible from that quaint and antique drainage system which you are applying to your face?
Sir Thomas Beecham to a trombonist after a less-than-impressive performance

How do you know when it's time to tune your bagpipes?
Tom O'Connor

Playing the bagpipes for the first time is like having sex with an octopus.
Andrew McDonald

Mick Jagger could play a tuba from both ends.
Joan Rivers

The best way to tell if a bagpipe is out of tune is to have someone blow into it.
Stephen Arnott

There's only one thing worse than a clarinet – two clarinets.
Ambrose Bierce

The chief objection to playing wind instruments is that it prolongs the life of the player.
George Bernard Shaw

Thank you. And now would you please pull the chain?
Sir Thomas Beecham to a tuba player who disappointed him

The inventor of the bagpipes was inspired when he saw a man carrying an indignant asthmatic pig under his arm.

Unfortunately, the man-made sound never equalled the purity of that made by the pig.
Alfred Hitchcock

How is it possible for Bob Dylan to play the harmonica professionally for thirty years and still show no sign of improvement?
David Sinclair

The best place to listen to bagpipes being played in Scotland is London.
Archie McLeod

Twelve highlanders and a bagpipe make a rebellion.
Sir Walter Scott

The British Rock and Pop Awards have the lasting importance of someone breaking wind in a hurricane.
Clive James

The difference between a bagpipe and an onion is that nobody cries when you chop up a bagpipe.
Henry Quelp

Billie Holiday doesn't need any horns. She sounds like one anyway.
Miles Davis

The reason bagpipers walk when they play is to get away from the noise.
Spike Milligan

I've played the harmonica ever since I was big enough to defend myself.
Herb Shriner

My father once tried to play 'Flight of the Bumblebee' on the tuba. He blew his liver through the horn.
Woody Allen

My brother plays the French horn so badly it comes out sounding like Greek.
Terry Martin

The best thing I can say about bagpipes is that they don't smell too.
Brendan Behan

Quit Your Lowdown Ways

Rod Stewart is so mean it hurts him to go to the bathroom.
Britt Ekland

Ireland is such a corrupt country, next year Chris de Burgh's *son* is going to win Miss World.
Fran Dempsey

When I get down on my knees it is not to pray.
Madonna

Rhianna wears her dresses cut to see-level.
Fran Casey

George Michael was arrested for exposing himself in a toilet. Is this what you'd call a flash in the pan?
Joe Morrison

Van Morrison wouldn't authorise a journalist to write his shopping list.
Brenda Power

Michael Bolton said he wants to be an opera singer. That's great because it means my Dad and me can now both hate the same kind of music.
Conan O'Brien

Don't judge Cher by her clothes. There isn't enough evidence.
Bob Hope

You know what you do when you shit? Singing is the same, except upwards.
Enrico Caruso

Irish songs are about fucking, fighting and drinking – the important things in life.
Shane MacGowan

Oh Calcutta is the sort of show that gives pornography a bad name.
Clive James

All men are jackals but you need one to protect you from the rest of them.
Marlene Dietrich

Somebody should clip Sting around the head and tell him to stop using that ridiculous Jamaican accent.
Elvis Costello

The majority of Irish men are bastards. And they're fucking useless in bed.
Mary Coughlan

Def Leppard are the George Bush of rock 'n' roll.
Jon Steinman

Some man sent me condoms and a pair of underpants in the post. He should have been more specific. I'm not sure what he wanted.
Martine McCutcheon

Beatlemania is like the frenzied dancing of voodoo worshippers and the bodily writhings of converts among primitive evangelical sects in the southern states of America.
Dr. F. Casson

He can't sing a lick. He makes up for his vocal shortcomings with the weirdest animations just short of an aborigine's mating dance.
Jack O'Brien on Elvis Presley

I want to have a baby and I want Peter Jennings to be the father. I know he's married but we could just have a cheap and tawdry affair.
Sheena Easton

I'm erasing all your harmonies from my tape and I'm marrying Carrie Fisher next week.
Paul Simon to Art Garfunkel in 1983

Robbie Williams has a lot to answer for. Nowadays every trained chimp in the charts feels they too can have a stab at credible solo stardom.
Tanya Sweeney on post-Westlife Bryan McFadden

Somebody present at the Band-Aid recording said he hadn't seen such competition for lines since the great coke shortage of '73.
Eamonn McCann

I used to sit in the front row at Tina Turner concerts so I could look up her dress.
Madonna

I bit the head off a live bat the other night. It was like eating a Crunchie wrapped in chamois leather.
Ozzy Osbourne

I get the main ideas for songs from the supermarket. I have a talent for eavesdropping. It's amazing what you learn while waiting for your fruit juice.
Morrissey

I want to grow old disgracefully.
Sandie Shaw

Our ambition is to pollute and destroy the world.
Axl of Guns'n'Roses

Oh Sister

Her singing was something between the sound of a rat drowning, a lavatory flushing and a hyena devouring her afterbirth in the Appalachian mountains under a full moon.
Auberon Waugh on a colleague

Beyonce is a bitch. I hope she gets bit on the arse by whatever animal she's wearing.
Pink

The idea with modern girlbands is that they look like models and dance like zombies: Singing is an optional extra.
Brenda Kehoe

She was a singer who had to take every note above A with her eyebrows.
Montague Glass

One Kate Bush is worth two in the hand.
Graffiti

Madam, there you sit with that magnificent instrument between your legs and all you can do is scratch it.
Arturo Toscanini to a woman playing the cello

She'd resemble Wagner if only she looked a bit more feminine.
Osbert Sitwell on Dame Ethel Smyth

Ladies of the choir, I want you to sound like 22 women having babies without chloroform.
John Barbirolli

Diana Ross is a piece of liquorice in shoes. When she walks into a pool hall, they chalk her *head*.
Joan Rivers

It's not possible for a family to be as uniformly beautiful as the Corrs. I often feel there must be a Pat Corr hidden away somewhere, a guy with sausage-like fingers who repeatedly asks to be allowed play the mandolin and keeps getting knocked on the head and told 'No' before being put back in the cupboard.
Jack Dee

So Victoria Beckham got pregnant a few World Cups ago. Well it's nice to see David had *something* on target.
Angela Miller

Happiness can be an old woman falling off a donkey.
Morrissey

The good thing about The Spice Girls is that you can look at them with the sound turned down.
George Harrison

Sinead O'Connor acts like she developed her personality in a car accident.
Colin Fraser

Madonna has a gold tooth in her mouth and shit around her eyes. She looks like Beetlejuice.
Mark Wahlberg

Madonna is a gay man trapped in a woman's body.
Boy George

What they call Rosalind Russell I can't repeat but it rhymes with 'witch.' And you'll find her in a kennel.
Ethel Merman

Is there any beginning to her talent?
Joe Duffy on Geri Halliwell

Cher has finally admitted she was sixty. But she didn't say when.
Rodney Dangerfield

Janet Jackson has the sort of smile you just know she's rehearsed and rehearsed. Think of a second-hand car dealer trying to beat an NTC deadline and then add about 1000 watts.
Paul Byrne

She couldn't chew gum and walk straight at the same time, never mind write a book.
Liam Gallagher on Posh Spice after her autobiography appeared in 2001

When Maria Callas carried a grudge, she planted it, nursed it, fostered it, watered it, and watched it grow to sequoia size.
Harold Schonberg

There have been times when I've prayed for a bus to hit me so I'd have an excuse not to perform.
Linda Ronstadt

I give you – the two and only Dolly Parton.
Rodney Dangerfield

Why do all my girlfriends look alike? It all goes back to Marilyn Monroe being an early masturbation fantasy.
Rod Stewart

David Bowie once admitted to me that he always wanted to be Judy Garland.
Elton John

When Maria Callas sings, she hits notes so high that only dogs can hear them. As far as I'm concerned that's the dog's problem.
Bernard Manning

Just Like Tom Thumb's Blues

Cilla Black's voice is like labour pain set to music.
Bob Monkhouse

Duran Duran remind me of a baroque art-rock bubblegum broadcast on a frequency understood only by female teenagers and bred fieldmice.
Mark Coleman

If human genitalia could sing, they'd sound like Enya.
Dylan Moran

Simon Cowell is a pompous little prick who walks like he has a stick stuck up his arse.
Sharon Osbourne

Amy Winehouse looked like a campaign poster for neglected horses.
Frankie Boyle

Tom Waits is like the tramp who wandered in through the back door with a bottle of whiskey in his tattered coat pocket, his lyrics written in the mud between his fingernails.
Robert Wilonsky

Sleeping with George Michael would be like having sex with a groundhog.
Boy George

Enrique Iglesias is like a disoriented gannet swimming away from the Exxon Valdez oil spill straight into Peter Stringfellow's discarded thong.
Mark Lamarr

Ronnie Drew's voice always sounded like he was gargling with pebbles.
Gerry Ryan

Simon Cowell telling people they have no talent is like poop telling vomit it stinks.
Comic Dog

Rap music sounds like someone feeding a rhyming dictionary to a popcorn popper.
Tom Robbins

Beethoven's 7th Symphony is like a lot of yaks jumping about.
Sir Thomas Beecham

When Jack Benny played the violin, it sounded as if the strings were still back in the cat.
Fred Allen

Listening to the Fifth Symphony of Ralph Vaughan Williams is like staring at a cow for 45 minutes.
Aaron Copland

Barbra Streisand looks like a cross between an aardvark and an albino rat, surmounted by a platinum-coated horse bun.
John Simon

Barry Manilow's voice sounds like a bluebottle caught in the curtains.
Jean Rook

John Lennon was like a dog who had rabies: you never knew when he was going to jump up and bite you.
Pezo Hoffmann

The closest equivalent to Roseanne Barr's singing the National Anthem was my cat being neutered.
Johnny Carson

You have to have smelt a lot of cow manure before you can sing like a hillbilly.
Hank Williams

I can compare *Le Carnival Romain* by Berlioz to nothing but the gibberings of a big baboon over-excited by a dose of alcoholic stimulus.
George T. Strong

Irving Berlin had a voice that sounded like a hoarse tomcat with its tail in a clothes wringer.
Bob Hope

The sound of a harpsichord resembles that of a bird-cage played with toasting forks.
Sir Thomas Beecham

Yoko Ono's voice sounds like an eagle being goosed.
Ralph Novak

The third movement of Bartok's Fourth Quartet began with a dog howling at midnight, proceeded to imitate the regurgitations of the less refined type of water-closet, and concluded with the cello reproducing the scratch of an ungreased wheelbarrow.
Clarence Darrow

I love Wagner, but the music I prefer is that of a cat hung up by its tail outside a window and trying to stick to the panes of glass with its claws.
Charles Baudelaire

We're being told Madonna is like a modern-day Marilyn Monroe. Comparing Madonna with Marilyn Monroe is like comparing Raquel Welch to the back end of a bus.
Boy George

Bob Dylan has a voice that sounds like a malfunctioning cistern.
George Byrne

I can sing as well as Fred Astaire can act.
Burt Reynolds

Mick Jagger moves like a parody between a majorette girl and Fred Astaire.
Truman Capote

Kate Moss is like the product of mating Patti Smith with a Hoover vacuum cleaner.
Dave McGee

Bryan Ferry sings like he's throwing up.
Andrew O'Connor

His vibrato sounded like he was driving a tractor over ploughed fields with weights tied to his scrotum.
Spike Milligan

Eamon Dunphy has a singing voice that makes Lee Marvin sound like Pavarotti.
Joe Jackson

Canned music is like audible wallpaper.
Alistair Cooke

Wearing tight striped pants, he looked like a bifurcated marrow.
Clive James on Rod Stewart

Beethoven reminds me of a man driving a car with the handbrake on but stubbornly refusing to stop even though there's a strong smell of burning rubber.
Colin Wilson

Robbie Williams has been voted Sexiest Man Alive. That's a bit like picking Jackie Healy-Rae as the greatest statesman in the history of civilisation.
Ian O'Doherty

To hear Tom Jones sing Sinatra's 'My Way' is roughly akin to watching Tab Hunter play *King Lear*.
Sheridan Morley

Adele's voice is like asthma set to music.
Michael Harkness

The harpsicord sounds like two skeletons copulating on a tin roof.
Sir Thomas Beecham

The sort of music a pederast might hum while raping a choirboy.
Marcel Proust on Faure's 'Romances san Paroles'

The Sydney Opera House looks like a broken Pyrex casserole dish in a brown cardboard box.
Clive James

Bob Dylan resembles nothing so much as an alcoholic lumberjack on a Saturday night out in some Saskatchewan backwater.
Allan Jones

He had a face like a police identikit photograph.
Richard Baker on Roger Daltrey

I would define jazz as sound having an epileptic fit.
Tommy Tiernan

Prince looked like a dwarf that fell into a vat of pubic hair.
Boy George

Lloyd Webber's music is everywhere but then so is AIDS.
Malcolm Williamson

Cher looks like a bag of tattooed bones in a sequined slingshot.
Andrea Jarski

If by some miracle I met John Lennon I'm sure he'd be no different to me. Just some chancer on the piss who managed to string a few chords together and sell a lot of records.
Noel Gallagher

The other night I thought Nancy had one of George Burns' records on but it turned out to be a spoon caught in the garbage disposal.
Ronald Reagan

What's the difference between Robbie Williams and a supermarket trolley? A supermarket trolley has a mind of its own.
Chris McLachlan

Playing Bop is like scrabble with all the vowels missing.
Duke Ellington

Jon Bon Jovi looks like he's got a brick dangling from his willy. And a food-mixer making puree of his tonsils.
Paul Lester

Richard Clayderman is to piano-playing what David Soul is to acting. He makes Jacques Loussier sound like Bach.
Richard Williams

Going to the opera, like getting drunk, is a sin that carries its own punishment with it.
Hannah More

Madonna has been made up to look like an aspiring bag lady with the skin of a pneumonia victim.
Time magazine on Who's That Girl?

Denis Norden's singing voice resembles a heron with its legs caught.
Frank Muir

The Virgin Prunes looked like a bunch of pre-Raphaelite serial killers.
Ferdia MacAnna

Throwing a football is comparable to painting a canvas. The difference is that Van Gogh didn't paint 'The Potato Eaters' with Mean Joe charging at him from the blind side.
Jim Plunkett

I have a voice like a goose farting in a fog.
Billy Connolly

Wedding Song

When Michael Jackson married Lisa-Marie Presley there wasn't a wet eye in the house.
Dan Naughton

It was years before I realised what was wrong with my marriage to Debbie Reynolds. *Everything*.
Eddie Fisher

Liza Minnelli's wedding reception was the night of a thousand facelifts.
Tina Brown

A woman has written a book claiming she was married to Bob Dylan for six years. Everyone thinks the marriage was a secret but it wasn't. It's just that when Dylan told people about it, they couldn't understand what he was saying.
Conan O'Brien

Mozart was happily married but his wife wasn't.
Victor Borge

I got fed up of being turned down by birds in the pub.
Eric Clapton explaining why he decided to get married).

If a Smiths fan went out and shot Maggie Thatcher I'd marry that person.
Morrissey

Jerry Lee Lewis has been married twenty times. He gets married on a Tuesday and by Thursday they've found his wife dead in a swimming pool.
Denis Leary

When Barbra Streisand's husband looked at her face the morning after the wedding he said, 'For Christ's sake, sing'
John Grossman

What everybody needs in the music industry is a wife. I wish I had a wife.
Chrissie Hynde

The trouble about women is that they get all excited about nothing and then marry it.
Cher

I'm more afraid of marriage than death.
Shakira

Marriage is a long dull meal with the dessert at the beginning.
Dean Martin

James Brolin marrying Barbra Streisand was a smart move. It's one way for an ageing TV star to get back in the spotlight

without going the OJ Simpson route.
Morey Amsterdam

I can't come to your wedding because of a previous engagement, mom, but I promise to be at your next one.
Liza Minnelli to Judy Garland before her fifth wedding

Being married to a beautiful girl is expensive because you also have to hire a cook.
Sammy Davis Jr

Being married to Greg Allman was like going to Disneyland on acid. You know you had a good time but can't remember what you did.
Cher

Four must be my unlucky number. I married my fourth husband in 1964 and four weeks was all I could stand with the fella.
Ethel Merman

Marriage licences should be renewed annually like dog licences.
Rod Stewart

I had to set my hair on fire to make news. You only had to get married.
Telegram from Michael Jackson to Elton John in 1984

Get dressed. We're going to Tijuana.
Ike Turner's marriage proposal to Tina

The majority of husbands remind me of an orangutan trying to play the violin.
Honore de Balzac

Marriage to Bob Dylan wouldn't have worked out for me. I was too political and he lied too much.
Joan Baez

When John Lennon got a picture of my wedding to Linda he crossed out the word 'wedding' and put in 'funeral' instead.
Paul McCartney

It was a bit like going on vacation with your ex-wife.
Andrea Glynn on the reunion of Simon & Garfunkel

Ike Turner is single again. His thirteenth wife has left him. She came home unexpectedly and caught him punching out another woman.
Jay Leno

When you start to feel married, that's when you should divorce.
Mick Jagger

The worst thing Michael Jackson was ever guilty of was causing middle-aged drunk people at weddings to try and do the moonwalk.
Billy Connolly

When Michael Jackson married the Presley girl a friend asked me what I was giving the happy couple. I replied, 'About two months.'
Rodney Dangerfield

It Ain't Me, Babe

From the waist up, Buddy Holly looked more like Buddy Holly's accountant than a pop singer.
Cliff Richard

I like Dolly Parton but couldn't class her as a friend. She's too busy being Dolly Parton all the time. I'd find that very exhausting.
Graham Norton

They broke the mould when they made Michael Jackson – every time.
Jay Leno

David wanted the basic, good old-fashioned English rock star marriage in which hubby lances his way boldly and beautifully around the globe, free as an eagle while wifey stays happily home on the nice suburban Home Counties estate, studying macrobiotics and macramé and raising babies in post-Woodstock Victorian virtue,
Angie Bowie

I don't think he was ever born to be a rock 'n' roll star. He was probably born to be chairman of Watford Football Club. And now he's beginning to *look* like the chairman of Watford Football club.
Rod Stewart on Elton John in 1977

I'm capable of being a rock 'n' roll star and the chairman of Watford Football Club, and I sell more records than Rod Stewart. Anyway, he should stick to grave-digging, 'cos that's where he belongs, six feet under.
Elton John in reply

You can dress up a turd so much but it still looks like a turd.
Julian Cope on George Michael

People's images of me range from vilification to sanctification. Both piss me off.
Bob Geldof

The last time Cher had surgery they made a new person out of the bits that were left over.
Joan Rivers

Madonna is so hairy, when she lifted up her arm I thought Tina Turner was in her armpits.
Joan Rivers

Some days you wake up and you're Barbra Streisand.
Courtney Love

The reason I drink is because when I'm sober I think I'm Eddie Fisher.
Dean Martin

There's been three big phases in my celebrity status. With the Boomtown Rats it was Bob the Gob, then with the Live Aid thing it was Bob the God. Then it settled down to a general omnipresence.
Bob Geldof

When I was young I was portrayed as the epitome of the swinging chick who dated handsome guys. In reality I felt like the last remaining virgin in London.
Lulu

People never talk about my music. They just count how many pairs of knickers there are on the stage.
Tom Jones

No one writes about the clever little twists I put into my songs. All they're concerned about is the women in my life, how much I drink and how such money I've got. But those who've scribbled with the crooked nib will one day have to answer to that great editor in the sky.
Rod Stewart

Madonna's lipstick lesbianism and sado-masochism and all the rest of it was just a cover for the fact that she was a rather lonely woman in her thirties who wanted a baby.
Andrew Neil

Wagner: a beautiful sunset which one mistook for a dawn.
Claude Debussy

If I go into a village grocer's they all act real scared. What do they expect – that I'll rape their daughters or stick a needle in my arm?
Mick Jagger

There's nothing I wouldn't say to Julie Andrews' face – both of them.
Rock Hudson

Thank God I'm not me.
Bob Dylan

Knockin' on Heaven's Door

If life was fair, Elvis would still be alive and all his impersonators dead.
Johnny Carson

By the time Beethoven died, he was so deaf he thought he was an artist.
Pat McCormick

If you want to see what Cher will look like when she's dead, all you have to do is look at her now.
Joan Rivers

It's a sobering thought that when Mozart was my age he'd been dead for two years.
Tom Lehrer

Marilyn Manson was on tour with Courtney Love but it didn't work out. Apparently Courtney scared off all the Satan worshippers.
Bill Maher

Sting – where is thy death?
Joe Queenan

I lost my faith in rock stars in 1971 when I discovered The Grateful Dead took out life insurance.
Paddy Woodworth

The words I want on my tombstone are 'Fuck you'.
Shane MacGowan

The Everly Brothers died ten years ago.
Don Everly at their farewell concert in 1973

Somebody dug up John Lennon's corpse the other day. He was decomposing.
Dennis Keough

Glenn Miller became a legend in his lifetime because of his early death.
Nicholas Parsons

Thank God he won't be singing at my funeral!
Spike Milligan after hearing of Harry Secombe's death in 2001

Elvis Lives. And they've gone and buried the poor bugger.
Graffiti

Brahms' *Requiem* is patiently borne only by the corpse.
George Bernard Shaw

Frank Sinatra's the kind of guy who, when he dies, he's gonna go up to heaven and give God a bad time for making him bald.
Marlon Brando

I hope he saved some of my money to pay for his funeral.
Maria Callas after hearing her agent had died

My chief objection to the playing of wind instruments is that it prolongs the life of the player.
George Bernard Shaw

There's no justice in the world. They killed John Lennon and let Des O'Connor live.
Roy Brown

Damn Jimi Hendrix for beating me to the grave.
Janis Joplin

No operatic tenor has yet died soon enough for me.
Sir Thomas Beecham

Knowing me, I'll probably get busted at my own funeral.
Jimi Hendrix

Elvis died the day he went into the army.
John Lennon

'Spinning Wheel' by Blood Sweat and Tears is music to commit voluntary euthanasia by.
Simon Hoggart

You better not die, you bitch, or I'll fucking kill you.
Ike Turner to Tina after she'd attempted suicide as a result of being brutalised by him

The only times I've felt like killing myself have been in Ireland.
Sinead O'Connor

Men don't really believe women exist. Marilyn Monroe died of this.
Lucy Ellman

'Aria' is Italian for 'A song that won't end in your lifetime.'
Dave Barry

The next time I get played on Radio 2 will probably be the day I die.
Midge Ure

How dare he die in my week!
Janis Joplin on Dwight Eisenhower, whose death deprived her of the cover of Newsweek in 1969.

I've considered suicide 183 times. The first time the idea of it appealed to me was when I was eight.
Morrissey

Rock 'n' roll is dead. It's a toothless old woman.
David Bowie in 1975

What would Elvis say if he was reincarnated? 'I've been dead over forty years and I still look better than Keith Richards!'
Garry Bushell

The Times They Are A-Changing

Elvis Presley started his career looking like Stan Laurel and ended it looking like Oliver Hardy.
Ben Stennett

I'm getting old. I watched Madonna writhe around on the hood of a car in a video the other day and all I could think was: That's really going to drive up her insurance premium.
Jon Stewart

The good thing about today's music is that if the acoustics are bad, you don't know it.
Hal Roach

Old age is when you walk into a record store and everything you like is marked down to £1.99.
Jack Simmons

The good thing about the iPod is that you can now store 10,000 songs in there – or two Pink Floyd tracks.
Stuart Maconie

Madonna used to sing songs like 'Papa Don't Preach.' Now it's more like, 'Fuck me, fuck me, fuck me.'
Sir Mix-a-Lot

I've been accused of being a racist. Nonsense. I was a friend of Michael Jackson even when he was black.
Joan Rivers

After a few boring years, socially meaningful rock 'n roll died out. It was replaced by disco, which offers no guidance to any form of life outside the lichen family.
Dave Barry

Being a famous singer made it possible for me to get insulted in places where the average Negro could never hope to be insulted.
Sammy Davis Jr.

Modern music is three farts and a raspberry, orchestrated.
John Barbirolli

Las Vegas gets a bad rap. When you think of it you think: Gamblers and hookers. It's more of a family place now. It's gamblers, hookers and hookers' kids.
Barry Manilow

A record I made was in the shops so long, the hole in the middle healed up.
Andy Cameron

Where else but in America could a poor black boy like Michael Jackson grow up to be a rich white woman?
Red Buttons

The worst part of being gay in the 20th century is all that damn disco music to which one has to listen.
Quentin Crisp

The eighties were a strange time for music. You went from Sid Vicious wanting to kick your bollocks to Boy George wanting to kiss them.
Ally McCoist

A name from ancient history, a broken star touring the cabaret spots to bored audiences, singing a song that won the Eurovision nobody was sure when.
Orna Mulcahy on Johnny Logan in 1987

The only reason The Pogues started playing the kind of music we did was because no other fucker was doing it.
Shane MacGowan

Madonna started off as a guttersnipe and now she's acting like the Queen Mother.
James Sherwood

What do you get when you play New Age music backwards? New Age music.
Ken Baldwin

Parsifal is the kind of opera that starts at six o'clock and after it has been going three hours, you look at your watch and it says 6.20.
David Randolph

People are wrong when they say that opera isn't what it used to be. It is. That's what's wrong with it.
Noel Coward

Gershwin asked me if his music would still be played in a hundred years time. I told him it would if he was still around.
Oscar Levant

Modern music is the noise made by deluded speculators picking through the slagpile.
Henry Pleasants

History, it is said, repeats itself first as tragedy and then as farce. In the case of Jive Bunny and the Nastermixers, it repeats itself like a bad Spanish dinner.
J.D.Considine

One good thing about playing a piece of modern music is that if you make a mistake, no one notices.
Gordon Brown

Musical talent today means looking good while lip-synching to a cover version.
Joe O'Shea

Sinead O'Connor is like a stopped clock. She's right twice a day.
Liam Fay

Modern music hasn't been around too long, and hopefully won't be.
Victor Borge

When you're about 35 years old, something terrible always happens to music.
Steve Race

Something is Happening Here But You Don't Know What It Is, Do You Mr Jones?

The latest rumour is that Britney Spears is pregnant again. It turns out it wasn't planned. She said it happened when she was sitting on a limo seat.
Jay Leno

Pavarotti was very difficult to pass at the net in tennis - even when he wasn't playing.
Peter Ustinov

I used to think Kanye West was a tube station near Uxbridge.
Jonathan Ross

Leonard Cohen was born Leonard Nimoy in Toronto in 1934. He grew his ears long in the sixties in protest against the Vietnam war and withdrew to the Greek island of Vulcan. His

first book of poetry, *I'm a Lumberjack*, remained in the Ontario Top Ten for 57 years.
Kevin McAleer

What would you call a blues singer with half a brain? Gifted.
Henny Youngman

The reason I close my eyes when I'm singing is because I have the words of the songs written on the inside of my eyelashes.
Christy Moore

So where's the Cannes Film Festival being held this year?
Christina Aguilera

Don't confuse fame with success. One is Madonna, the other Helen Keller.
Erma Bombeck

If Donny Osmond had an idea it would die of loneliness.
Kim Forsythe

The music of Stravinsky is just Bach on the wrong notes.
Sergei Prokofiev

Berlioz says nothing in his music but he says it magnificently.
James Gibbon Huneker

I didn't have any preconceptions about them. I thought they were UB40.
Eamon Dunphy on U2 before writing their biography.

The music is in German. You would not understand it.
Oscar Wilde

I didn't write the song 'I Write the Songs'.
Barry Manilow

I don't mind what language an opera is sung in as long as it's one I don't understand.
Edward Appleton

The reason some people don't like your music is the same reason other people do.
Kirsty McColl

It sold 6½ million records and there's not a decent track on it.
Rod Stewart on 'Blondes Have More Fun'

Mine was the kind of piece in which nobody knew what was going on, including the conductor and the critics. Consequently, I got pretty good notices.
Oscar Levant

Musical people are so absurdly unreasonable. They always want one to be perfectly dumb at the very moment when one is longing to be absolutely deaf.
Oscar Wilde

What the fuck do composers do? All the good music's already been written by people with wigs and stuff.
Frank Zappa

You don't need any brains to listen to music.
Luciano Pavarotti

You could put everything I know about men on the top of a pin and still have room for the Lord's Prayer.
Cher

I don't like country music but I don't denigrate those who do. And for people who like country music, 'denigrate' means 'put down'.
Bob Newhart

Mick Jagger never knew how to shake that boney little ass of his until he watched me strut on stage.
Tina Turner

Handel is so great and so simple that no one but a professional musician is unable to understand him.
Samuel Butler

He got off the song somehow and limped off amidst roars of silence from the audience.
P.G. Wodehouse

Rock journalism is people who can't write interviewing people who can't talk for people who can't read.
Frank Zappa

Frank Sinatra's idea of Paradise is a place where there are plenty of women and no newspapermen. He doesn't know it but he'd be better off if it was the other way round.
Humphrey Bogart

No, my brother was an only child.
Ringo Starr after being asked if he had any siblings

You write a hit the same way you write a flop.
Alan Jay Lerner

Madonna exercises to stop being depressed. If she didn't exercise she'd be depressed about not exercising.
Douglas Thompson

Even though I'm right-handed, I give left-handed handshakes to throw people.
Prince

I've finally figured out why operas are all in a foreign language. It's so the guy who wrote them would understand them.
Gene Perret

There are three important rules governing the writing of hit songs. The problem is, nobody knows what they are.
Barry Manilow

At my shows, people don't know whether to fuck or kill each other. That's the way I like it.
Marilyn Manson

The fact that Mel C forgave me for calling her a fat lesbian so often leads me to believe she isn't one after all.
Graham Norton

Rock 'n' roll is a combination of good ideas dried up by fads, terrible junk, hideous failings in taste and judgment, moments

of unbelievable clarity and invention, pleasure, fun, vulgarity, excess, novelty and utter enervation.
Greil Marcus

Knocked Out Loaded

Just because I cut the heads off dolls they say I must hate babies. It's not true. I just hate dolls.
Alice Cooper

I heard a rumour that Dawn French was busted for drug smuggling at Cardiff airport. Apparently when she bent over, the customs officer saw 50 pounds of crack.
Aled Lewis

The Beatles were so high on drugs when they recorded 'Yellow Submarine' they even let Ringo sing on it.
Bill Hicks

I hear Keith Richards has called on young people to stop taking drugs. They have to, Keith. After you there are none left.
Denis Leary

All the bad things I ever did in my life were due to alcohol. Sober I would never have urinated at the Alamo at nine o'clock in the morning in a woman's evening dress.
Ozzy Osbourne

Never take ecstacy, beer, bacardi, weed, xanax and valium on the same day. It makes it difficult to sleep.
Eminem

A typical day in the life of a heavy metal musician consists of a round of golf followed by an AA meeting.
Billy Joel

I tried to give up drugs by drinking.
Lou Reed

Seattle's new rock 'n' roll museum was inspired by Jimi Hendrix. The first patron to choke on his own vomit gets a free syringe.
Craig Kilborn

Diana Ross entered an alcohol rehab centre because she said she wanted to 'clear up some personal issues.' Before going on tour. Like being able to stand up on stage.
Joan Rivers

Elvis was pretty far gone the first time I saw him. It made sense when women threw their bras at him. He needed them.
Tom Kenny

Ozzy Osbourne was invited to the White House to meet George Bush when he was president. It just goes to show you that if you do a lot of controlled substances and talk like a three-year-old you can go really far in America. Ozzy's doing okay too.
Greg Poops

Having guzzled his way through the day at Stansted and slurped his fill of wine on the flight, there were some difficult moments for Shane MacGowan on touchdown at Dublin. He had to walk all the way from his aeroplane seat to the Arrivals area without a drink.

Liam Fay

Happily married musicians fall in love on the road all the time. It's something to do along with drinking too much, taking too many drugs and supergluing the tour manager's bed to the ceiling.

Robin Eggar

Every time you read about some famous person overdosing on drugs they're always really talented, like Janis Joplin or Jimi Hendrix or John Belushi. The people you *want* to overdose never would. Motley Crue would never overdose. Or New Kids on the Block.

Denis Leary

I only drink moderately. I keep a case of Moderately in my dressing-room.

Dean Martin

I said no to drugs but they just wouldn't listen.

Keith Moon

Sometimes when I'm flying over the Alps I think: That's all the cocaine I sniffed.

Elton John

In our prime we had parties that Nero would have been ashamed to attend.

Ronnie Hawkins

In Manchester you either become a musician, a footballer, a drug dealer or work in a factory. And there aren't a lot of factories left.
Noel Gallagher

Pat Boone once told me drinking was slow poison. I said, 'Who's in a hurry?'
Dean Martin

I only ever get ill when I give up drugs.
Keith Richards

You're not drunk if you can lie on the floor without holding on.
Dean Martin

You don't form a band to drink milk.
Shane MacGowan

If you're going to get wasted, get wasted elegantly.
Keith Richards

When Paul McGuinness managed to get me a pint of beer when I was under the legal drinking age, I knew he was the man I wanted to manage U2.
The Edge

If you want to be in a pop group, you either become completely debauched and die of a drug overdose after a couple of years, or else you renounce everything and live like a nun. I've straddled them both.
Annie Lennox

I signed myself into the Betty Ford Clinic because I was sick and tired of being sick and tired.
Liza Minnelli

Infidels

Rock is really about dick and testosterone. I go see a band, I wanna fuck the guy. That's the way it is and that's the way it's always been.
Courtney Love

Ours is a group with built-in hate.
The Who in 1965

I'm interested in anything about revolt, disorder, chaos and any activity that has no meaning.
Jim Morrison

In all the time I was on the road I must have laid a million girls. A few boys too, and the odd goat. The goats were all right but you had to go round the other end to kiss them.
Ronnie Hawkins

Once you make your peace with authority you become authority.
Jim Morrison

I am the slime from your video.
Frank Zappa

I lie a lot. It can be extremely useful.
Morrissey

At school I was Minister for Torture. I put dustbin lids over kids' heads and banged them for half an hour. I got stinging nettles and rubbed their balls with them, tweaked their nipples and generally abused them. That was before I read the Marquis de Sade. Sadism is a fairly normal condition.
Shane MacGowan

Be childish. Be irresponsible. Be disrespectful. Be everything this society hates.
Malcolm McLaren

I smash guitars because I like them. I usually do it when they're at their best.
Pete Townshend

I found my inner bitch and ran with her.
Courtney Love

People think that in some former life I was a debauched rugby player or that I've got a stream of illegitimate children cluttering up some home on a hillside.
Morrissey

I'm the type of guy who'd sell you a rat's asshole for a wedding ring.
Tom Waits

We used to rob houses when we were on the way up. How we ever managed to do any burgling I don't know. We were all off our tits on drugs.
Noel Gallagher

I believe in a prolonged derangement of the senses in order to attain the unknown.
Jim Morrison

My success comes mainly from a desire to fuck with people.
Madonna

I hate all cunts, all journalists, television personalities, Fine Gael fuckers and Mark Lamarr.
Shane MacGowan

I'm a severe critic. If a person has a hole in their sock, they crumble before me.
Morrissey

We are the people our mothers warned us against.
John Lennon

We're the world's ugliest band. When we play, I expect to find puke in the aisles.
Bobby Colombey of Blood, Sweat and Tears

I was such an intellectual idiot as a young man that people were convinced if they talked to me I'd quote Genesis and bolts of lightning would descend from the sky. As a result, I was never kissed behind the bicycle sheds.
Morrissey

My parents were convinced that I would one day become Mr Average. Thirty years on I'm still an A1 freak.
Boy George

Wagner was a monster. He was anti-Semitic on Mondays and vegetarian on Tuesdays. On Wednesdays he was in favour of annexing Newfoundland. On Thursdays he wanted to sink Venice, and on Fridays he planned to blow up the Pope.
Tony Palmer

Johnny Rotten was Prince Charmless.
Michael Azzerad

My thing is this. If I'm sick enough to think it, then I'm sick enough to say it.
Eminem

Blood on the Tracks

That cocksucker. I could slit his jugular vein and suck his blood out.
Gary Crosby on his father Bing

You are a vampire. The God of a vampire business, a fake reality. A false God with no apparent soul of your own to feed on, and seemingly no bleedin' mind of your own either.
Sinead O'Connor to Louis Walsh in a letter to the Sunday Independent after he'd branded her a 'wasted talent'

Michael Jackson cut off his nose to spite his race.
Marvin Gaye

I made lobster recently. I'm squeamish so I didn't kill it. I just boiled some water and put on a Michael Bolton tape. It committed suicide.
Wendy Liebman

Yeah, I hit her. But I didn't hit her more than the average guy beats his wife.
Ike Turner when he was being interrogated for a 'domestic' with Tina

Manners, like hats, do not suit everyone, and I do not think they suit Frank Sinatra. He has found a straight left more effective. It goes better with his ties.
Tom Wiseman

Perhaps it was because Nero fiddled that they burned Rome.
Oliver Hereford

The Japanese Prime minister has apologised for Japan's part in world War 11. However, he still hasn't mentioned anything about karaoke.
David Letterman

I promote violence and I don't give a fuck.
Eminem

Make yourself at home, Frank, hit someone.
Don Rickles to Frank Sinatra in a nightclub

When my wife sings I make her go into the front garden. I don't want the neighbours to think I'm beating her.
Jackie Gleason

Can you imagine finding out you've married a man who wanted to watch an opera after Christmas dinner? You'd just have to beat him to death with your Sri Lankan rice steamer.
A.A. Gill

I like the film *The Getaway*. There's a violent pump-action shotgun scene that's worth watching for itself alone. And it shows you how to beat up your wife.
Shane MacGowan

Don't do violence, drugs or unprotected sex. Leave that to me.
Eminem

Ireland needs to be dragged into a bush and fucked.
Sinead O'Connor

The Eurythmics are nothing more than hippies with haircuts who stepped into the breach after punk. Please let them die painlessly in a plane crash.
Julie Birchill

Rock 'n' roll has always been full of shit. The whole idea of sex and drugs in the mix is a cliché. Someone has to put a bullet into its head.
Bono

There were times when people would actually run across the road to spit on him.
Terry Hooley on Feargal Sharkey

If I had a hammer I'd use it on Peter, Paul and Mary.
Howard Rosenberg

The sorrow of the Brighton bombing is that Thatcher escaped unhurt.
Morrissey

If you write anything nasty about me I'll come over to your place and blow up your toilet.
Courtney Love to a journalist

Sinatra's son must have been kidnapped by music critics.
Oscar Levant

Billy Connolly tells us he was an abused child. I think it all goes back to that woeful banjo-playing. Put in his parents' place, I'd probably have abused him too.
Bob Geldof

You know what I hate about punk? Tie-dyed T-shirts. I wouldn't wear a tie-dyed T-shirt unless it was dyed with the urine of Phil Collins and the blood of Jerry Garcia.
Kurt Cobain

Ike used to beat me with shoe stretchers that had metal rods in the middle. Then he would have sex with me. It was torture, pure and simple. One night he threw boiling hot coffee in my face, making my skin peel off. I ended up with third degree burns. Another time he used the poker from the fireplace, breaking my jaw and some ribs. When we went to the hospital he always said the same thing. I'd had an 'accident'.
Tina Turner

Motherfuckers come to my house and violate my property, my space. If I don't know you and my daughter's home and I feel you're any kind of a threat to me whatsoever, you're gonna get a gun in your face.
Eminem

Only a Pawn in Their Game

You can be up to your knees in white satin with gardenias in your hair and no sugar cane for miles around and still be working on a plantation in your mind.
Billie Holiday

Geri Halliwell arrived on my show with bus-loads of people, her own caterer. You feel like saying, 'You do relise you're paying for all of this, don't you? They're not here because they like you.' I don't think Geri got all that.
Graham Norton

In the old days the record business people used to say, 'We're in it for the lowest common denominator'. Now I feel we're way below that.
Van Morrison

Everyone who ever met Elvis Presley, it seems, is currently writing a book about him, from his numerologist to his under-gardener.
Martin Amis

I'm an instant star. Just add water and stir.
David Bowie

If Jimi Hendrix walked into a modern A&R office I don't think he'd get the red carpet. He'd be shown the door.
Bono

It used to be that you could send a wide-eyed girl in a smock to the Eurovision and come home with the top prize. These days nothing short of a full chorus line of bikini-clad supermodels and roller-skating elephants is enough to wow Europe.
Shane Hegarty

Elvis ate America before America ate him.
Bono

1 don't like my music but what is my opinion against millions of others?
Frederick Loewe

Judy Garland never saw a rainbow that wasn't manufactured in a studio. Her world was the Wicked Witch's world: Bubble, bubble, toil and trouble.
Ray Bolger

I'm not into the fame thing. Some people want it badly. Their only talent is for being recognised, so they bring an entourage and all that shite.
Sharleen Spiteri

Trust me, the record industry isn't particularly nice.
Simon Cowell

Brian Epstein didn't discover the Beatles. The Beatles discovered Brian Epstein.
Derek Norman

The music business has all the sincerity of a whore's kiss.
Sinead O'Connor

Disease of Conceit

Valentine's Day is the day you should be with the person you love the most. I understand Simon Cowell spent it alone.
Jay Leno

When you enter a room you have to kiss Frank Sinatra's ring. That's all right, but he keeps it in his back pocket.
Don Rickles

Oasis aren't arrogant. We just think we're the best band in the world.
Noel Gallagher

What's the first thing a guitarist does when he wakes up in the morning? He rolls over and introduces himself.
Bruno Kassel

Cliff Richard has love bites on his mirror.
Geoff Hyams

Anyone who needs 50,000 people a night to tell them they're okay has to have a bit missing.
Bono

Diana Ross thought she was the best singer in America. She wasn't even the best singer in The Supremes.
Colin Paterson

It was easy enough to make Al Jolson happy. You just had to cheer him for breakfast, applaud wildly for lunch and give him a standing ovation for dinner.
George Burns

Rossini addressed his letters to his mother as 'Mother of the famous composer'.
Robert Browning

All right then, you play Bach your way and I'll play him his.
Wanda Landowska to a fellow musician

I welcome him like I welcome cold sores. He's from England, he's angry, and he's got Mad Power Disease.
Paula Abdul on Simon Cowell

In the music industry a legend is someone with two consecutive hit singles.
Garry Trudeau

Diana Ross personally contacted the Channel 4 office to say how much she enjoyed appearing on my show. The reason she felt moved to call was because she thought her skin looked nice.
Graham Norton

I've only ever been in love with a beer bottle or a mirror.
Sid Vicious

I can hold a note as long as the Chase Manhattan Bank.
Ethel Merman

It takes him about two weeks after a tour to come back down to the planet Earth where the rest of us live.
Ali Hewson on her husband, Bono

Everyone's entitled to my opinion.
Madonna

I'm my own greatest fan.
David Bowie

I like your opera; I think I will set it to music.
Beethoven to a would-be composer

I had no disagreement with Barbra Streisand when I acted with her. I was merely exasperated by her tendency towards megalomania.
Walter Matthau

The Beatles were nothing before I arrived.
Noel Gallagher

If there isn't a camera trained on her somewhere she doesn't feel she exists.
Warren Beatty on Madonna

Elvis may have been the king of rock 'n roll but I'm the queen.
Little Richard

Joni Mitchell is about as modest as Mussolini.
David Crosby

The reason I look so well is because I fucked a lot.
Iggy Pop

I could fart in the bathtub and still be Number One.
Rod Stewart

The Pet Shop boys have never given a tinker's curse about being misunderstood. Adoration will do nicely, though.
The New Musical Express

Give me a laundry list and I will set it to music.
Gioacchino Rossini

I'm sure I even pose in my sleep.
Kylie Minogue

I enjoyed Eric Clapton more before he went on to be God.
Fran Casey

When Mariah Carey requires a drink, she simply cocks her head to one side like a puzzled dog, whereupon a small army of people run to her side with all sorts of juices and sodas, each bottle with a straw sticking out of it.
Graham Norton

A Hard Rain's a-Gonna Fall

Faure writes the sort of music a pederast might hum while raping a choirboy.
Marcel Proust

How many cunts are there is Oasis? I'll give you a clue. It's a number between zero and two.
Liam Gallagher

Victoria Beckham gives away all her old clothes to starving children. Let's face it – who else are they going to fit?
Pauline Calf

Why don't bass players ever catch a cold? Even a virus has some pride.
Bruno Kassel

No wonder Bob Geldof is such an expert on famine. He's been dining out on 'I Don't like Mondays' for thirty years.
Russell Brand

Bjork dances in the dark. And by the look of things, she dresses there too.
Richard Blackwell

Girls Aloud is five dogs with no balls.
Charlotte Church

Tina Turner is all legs and hair – with a mouth that could swallow not only a baseball stadium but the hot dog stand as well.
Laura Lee Davies

What is a harp but an over-sized cheese-slicer with cultural pretensions?
Denis Norden

Phil Collins is losing his hearing. Which makes him the luckiest man at a Phil Collins concert.
Simon Amstell

The kind of thing you do is just rock n' roll with lipstick.
John Lennon to David Bowie

When people said Michael Jackson had his father's nose, they probably meant it was something he picked up on the bathroom floor.
Angus Deayton

Diana Ross's desire for fame is like her hair. It keeps getting bigger.
Johnny Mathis

If all the people who were in John Lennon's class at school in Liverpool jumped over a wall at the same time there would be an earthquake.
George Best

A harpsichord is a bird-cage played with toasting forks.
Sir Thomas Beecham

I wish the Government would put a tax on pianos for the incompetent.
Edith Sitwell

His voice is a complete harangue in puffy diction and pure fervency. Under its propulsion the manufactured folk comes swarming to life like the energetic little creatures cavorting in a hunk of rotting ham illuminated by a microscope.
C.G. Burke on Elvis Presley

There are few moments during her recital when one can relax and feel confident that she will reach her goal, which is the end of the song.
Paul Hume on Margaret Truman

I never met you, but if I do you'll need a new nose and a supporter below. Westbrook Pegler, a guttersnipe, is a gentleman compared to you. You can take that as more of an insult than a reflection on your ancestry.
Margaret's father, President Harry S. Truman, in response

Frank Sinatra had the voice of a lifetime. Unfortunately it was *my* lifetime.
Bing Crosby

John Lennon's first girlfriend was called Thelma Pickles. Yoko Ono was an improvement on that – sort of.
Jay Leno

Everyone has a book in them – but not if you want to write it about Van Morrison.
Johnny Rogan

If a musician comes to your door, pay him and take your pizza.
Zig Ziglar

The Pogues have done for Irish music what Shane MacGowan did for dentistry.
Roy Guillane

Of course Boy George is gay. Did you not know Michael Jackson lost his other glove down his trousers?
Joan Rivers

Those people on the stage are making so much noise I can't hear a word you're saying.
Henry Parker Taylor to a talkative audience at a concert

When I was making *Notting Hill* I asked Julia Roberts to go out with me. I figured if she married Lyle Lovett we all had a chance.
Rhys Ifans

A musicologist is a person who can read music but can't hear it.
Sir Thomas Beecham

Jazz will endure as long as people hear it through their feet instead of their brains.
John Philip Sousa

Who's going to tell Stevie Wonder he's got a macramé plant holder on his head?
Joan Rivers

In the final analysis, opera is a poor substitute for baseball.
Los Angeles Herald

A *bodhrán* is a large, round, thick-skinned object, usually tight, which you have to hit with a stick to get anything out of. Elsewhere in the world this is known as a husband.
Terry Eagleton

There are two golden rules for an orchestra: start together and finish together. Nobody gives a damn what goes on in between.
Sir Thomas Beecham

Punk is a poisoned banquet of garbage.
Kevin Myers

The reason they call it rap music is because the C fell off at the printers.
Stephen Arnott

The only thing worse than a rock star is a rock star with a conscience.
Bono

Ever since Tim Henman came along, Cliff Richard is no longer England's best tennis player.
Simon Watson

Elvis Costello is a fat, boring, talentless, four-eyed git.
Shane MacGowan

It's arguable that Big Tom was more central to the modernisation of Irish society than the First Programme of Economic Expansion.
John Waters

There are three types of harmony: polyphonous, contrapuntal and lousy.
Bob Monkhouse

It must be great to be a man. They even get to pee standing up.
Madonna

The CIA are planning to cripple Iran by playing the Bee Gees latest album on special loudspeakers secretly parachuted into the country.
Record Mirror in 1988

Can't act. Can't sing. Slightly bald. Can dance a little.
Early screen test report on Fred Astaire

Opera is rap music for highbrows.
Graffiti

A lot of great bands over the years have been lost to higher education. That's why I hope the cost of tuition just keeps going up and up.
Gerard Cosloy

Cliff Richard's 'The Millennium Prayer' is the worst record of all time.
Simon Cowell

Jack Lemmon had to be an actor because the only other thing he could do was play the piano in a whorehouse.
Billy Wilder

I put Elvis Presley into movies because he had animal magnetism. I didn't give a damn about the music.
Hal Wallis

Fat men should not play the concertina.
Evelyn Waugh

People some times ask me have I any regrets in life. I only have one: A really awful haircut I got in the mid-eighties which launched a thousand Third Division soccer players.
Bono

Of all the affected, sapless, soulless, beginningless, endless, topless, bottomless, topsiturviest, tuneless doggerel of sounds I ever endured the deadness of, that eternity of nothing was the deadliest.
John Ruskin on a Wagner concert

Billy Ray Cyrus helped turn country music into beef jerky. Short on funk, low on nutrition and punishing to the digestion. Cyrus took his choreography from the Chippendales and his musical standards from the chipmunks.
Time magazine

Rock and roll at its core is merely a bunch of raving shit.
Lester Bangs

The greatest entertainer I've ever seen, but offstage a no-good son-of-a-bitch.
George Jessel on Al Jolson

Eurovision is a slow form of torture played out in front of 250 million people.
Lulu

The Sydney Opera House looks like a typewriter full of oyster shells.
Clive James

The film version of *Camelot* is the Platonic idea of boredom, roughly comparable to reading a three-volume novel in a language of which one knows only the alphabet.
John Simon

Elvis Presley has no discernible singing ability. His phrasing, if it can be called that, consists of the stereotyped variations that go with a beginner's aria in a bathtub.
Jack Gould in 1956

An English audience is like a good fuck. You hold hands with it for a while. You kiss it, you pet it, and then it pays you off.
Glenn Frey of the Eagles

When an opera star starts to sing her head off, she usually improves her appearance.
Victor Borge

The Beatles are so unbelievably horrible, so appallingly unmusical, so dogmatically insensitive to the magic of art, that they qualify as crowned heads of anti-music just as the impostor Popes went down in history as anti-Popes.
William F. Buckley

There have been more books written about Marilyn Monroe than there have been about World War II. And the comparison doesn't end there.
Billy Wilder

There's something ironic about a member of The Corrs opposing the dumping of toxic waste upon the Irish people.
Brendan O'Connor on Jim Corr's opposition to the Sellafield nuclear plant

The only sanction that will work against Israel is forcing them to take part in the Eurovision Song Contest.
George Galloway

Every supermarket has a dungeon housing a staff of deaf and dumb troglodytes trained to make random selections of cassettes for playing during business hours.
George Crosby

In my long career I have had guitar players that are as bad as you are but you're the only one making a living out of it.
Ronnie Hawkins to Bob Dylan after a concert in 1990

For a number of years now, audiences have had trouble trying to recognise which of his hits Bob Dylan is singing at his concerts. More recently it's become apparent he hasn't even a fucking clue himself.
Tommy Tiernan

If Yoko Ono's singing voice was a fight, they'd stop it.
Robert Wahl

Barry Manilow is bringing out a new range of nose-clippers. To the rest of us, they'll be more recognisable as garden shears.
Angus Deayton

You have a wonderful voice. Don't spoil it by singing.
Frank Sinatra to a novice

Million Dollar Bash

The idea that the Beatles were anti-materialistic is a myth. John and I used to sit down and say, 'Hey, let's write a swimming pool.'
Paul McCartney

'Imagine no possessions,' sang John Lennon. He owned a luxury apartment in New York solely to house his clothes.
Arthur Smith

Pop music is about stealing pocket money from children.
Ian Anderson

The Spice Girls are threatening to make a comeback. Why don't we just pay them what they want?
Alan Aitchinson

The X Factor is just karaoke with a bigger budget.
Katherine Lynch

Mariah Carey just wants to have funds.
Ellen DeGeneres

Not so much 'Another Brick in the Wall' as 'Another Prick with a Haul'.
Denys Djaeger on Roger Waters of Pink Floyd

Joan Collins is a commodity who would sell her own bowel movement.
Anthony Newley

If I give you ten dollars will you promise to get some singing lessons?
Bob Hope to a busker once

They're always saying I'm a capitalist pig. I suppose I am but it's good for my drumming.
Keith Moon

A woman was once looking for £4,000 off me for an antique. I told her I could buy a new one for that.
Rod Stewart

Neil Diamond is a girl's best friend.
Graffiti

Ike was so tight-fisted he used to fine me if I had a clasp missing off my dress or if my shoes weren't clean. By the end of some shows I ended up owing him money instead of making some.
Tina Turner

You know who'll make a fortune? The person who invents opera with subtitles.
Gene Perret

I was once offered $100,000 by a man who wanted me to insult him while he was making love to his wife.
Simon Cowell

A man criticised me once for making a million dollars when all I do is scream and holler. I told him he was right except for one thing: I scream and holler in key.
James Brown

You have no idea how much money it costs to look this cheap.
Dolly Parton

Michael Jackson offered a million bucks to some hospital in England to buy the bones of the Elephant Man. It seems to make sense – one freak trying to buy the remains of another one.
Sam Kinison

I've been famous since I was 18. The only difference now is that I've got enough money to get pissed all the time.
Shane MacGowan

Madonna has mentioned that I was important to her, and that's very satisfying. However, a cheque would be better.
Deborah Harry

Money makes you beautiful.
Madonna

With God on Our Side

When you meet this man you wonder. 'Why?' Did God knock at the wrong door by mistake and when it was opened by this scruffy Irishman, think, 'Oh, what the hell – he'll do'?
Life magazine on Bob Geldof

Bono was an atheist until he realised he was God.
Kay McLachlan

Madonna has a song called 'Like a Virgin.' The only thing Madonna will ever do like a virgin is give birth in a stable.
Bette Midler

If there's music in hell, it will be bagpipes.
Joe Tomelty

I enjoyed Eric Clapton more before he went on to be God.
Fran Casey

My mother used to pray that I would get cancer of the throat.
Maria Callas

I won't be happy until I'm as famous as God.
Madonna

The church has nothing in common with Christianity. I can remember being at school on Mondays and being asked, 'Did you go to church yesterday?' If you hadn't been, you literally had the arms twisted off you. It's 'We'll sever your head for your own good. You'll learn my son.'
Morrissey

If Jesus Christ was on earth today you'd probably find him in a gay bar in San Francisco.
Bono

History was written by winners. In the case of The Bible, the winner is God.
Marilyn Manson

God is a woman. Take it from there.
Bob Dylan

I wanted to stir some shit.
Sinead O'Connor on why she tore up a picture of The Pope on TV

Geri Halliwell has now brought out two volumes of her autobiography. That means she's published twice as many books as God. Or if you're Jewish, twice as many.
Mark Watson

I admire the Pope. I have a lot of respect for anyone who goes on tour without an album to promote.
Rita Rudner

Nuns are sexy.
Madonna

I was raised Catholic. Everybody who was raised Catholic hates religion.
Bruce Springsteen

We're more popular than Jesus.
John Lennon on The Beatles in the mid-sixties

Religion has become an industry. It has more in common with McDonalds than it does with me.
Bono

Mother Teresa was a tough old bird.
Bob Geldof

Religion is like a beautiful flower with sharp teeth. The tranquillity is always matched with moral goose-stepping. Once people have rigid beliefs they inevitably tend to look down on others and act like they've got God in their handbag.
Boy George

A half-naked dead man hangs in most homes and around our necks. The world's most famous murder-suicide was also the birth of a death icon – the blueprint for celebrity.
Marilyn Manson on Jesus

I once saw Al Greene. That was pretty close to it.
Elvis Costello after being asked if he believed in the supernatural

The idea of heaven is horrific. Life needs to end.
Morrissey

Jesus was all right but his disciples were thick.
John Lennon

Forever Young

Mick Jagger is now at that awkward age between *being* a Stone and *passing* one.
Jay Leno

Bill Wyman couldn't be here tonight. He's at the hospital attending the birth of his next wife.
Frank Worthington

Paul McCartney's hair dye is so obvious, when he last played at the Oscars it received an unofficial award as the evening's best special effect.
Philip Norman

Sometimes I feel old. I once asked a girl where she was when Elvis died and she said, 'I was in my mother.'
Paddy Moloney

Dickie Rock has now been in the music business for 142 years.
Ronan Collins

Mick Jagger told me his wrinkles were due to laughter, not age. 'Nothing is that funny,' I replied.
George Melly

We like to look sixteen and bored shitless.
David Johanssen of the New York Dolls

I'd be disappointed if I got to fifty. It would show a lack of resolve.
Morrissey

I'm not like Jane Fonda or any of those other women who say how fabulous they think it is to turn sixty. I think it's a crock of shit.
Cher

Better to burn out than to fade away.
Neil Young

The reason I manage to look so young is because I'm mentally retarded.
Deborah Harry

Stravinsky looks like a man who was potty-trained too early. And his music proves it.
Russell Hoban

Heralding themselves as prophets of doom for British youth culture, the Pet Shop Boys come across more like crybabies who haven't got their allowance.
Rob Hoeburger

Elvis Presley was nothing more than a silly little country boy who just happened to sing like a nigger.
Albert Goldman

Johnny said to his mother, 'Mummy, I want to be a drummer when I grow up'. 'Now Johnny,' his mum replied, 'You know you can't do both.'
Stephen Arnott

It's hard for boybands to realise that the vast majority of their audience are probably seven and eight years of age.
Paul Keogh

Rock and roll is the sound of grown men throwing tantrums.
Bono

Kids today are quite right about the music their parents listened to. Most of it was trash. And parents are quite right about what their young listen to. Most of that is trash too.
Gene Lees

You should never talk to anyone who listens to Mahler before they're 40.
Clive James

Jim Morrison was like a spoilt, clean-scrubbed schoolboy on his first day with drink.
John Cale

His wantonness isn't vicious. It's that of a great baby, rather tirelessly addicted to dressing himself up as Handel or Beethoven and making a prolonged and intolerable noise.
George Bernard Shaw on Johannes Brahms

Nobody younger than Bob Geldof was allowed near the stage because otherwise The Boomtown Rats would have seemed like a collection of brontosauri.
Morrissey on Band-Aid

Clean Cut Kids

I once shook hands with Pat Boone and my whole right side sobered up.
Dean Martin

Paul McCartney persists in making records that have all the beatnik wildness of a Neighbourhood Watch Meeting.
Victoria Segal

I'm sick of these new rock stars and their health kicks. Bruce Springsteen, Madonna, Mick Jagger. They're all pumped up and worked out. I like my rock stars the old-fashioned way. Skin and bones. Wasted away from drugs and drink. Open sores on their arms and scabs on their necks. Bad teeth. Big chip on their left shoulder. The most exercise I want them to get every morning is when they pull the vomit out of their throats from the night before.
Denis Leary

Did you hear Daniel O'Donnell got a girl into trouble? He told her mother she was smoking.
Brendan Grace

This house has quite a long and colourful history. It was built on an ancient Indian burial ground and was the setting for Satanic rituals, witch-burnings and five John Denver Christmas Specials.
The Simpsons

Olivia Newton-John is Australia's gift to insomniacs. She's the blonde leading the bland.
Minnie Riperton

The pop business today caters for boys and girls with squeaky clean hair, the wholesome smiles of *Blue Peter* presenters and the bite of nine-day-old tapioca pudding.
Philip Norman

Nice guys are a dime a dozen. Give me a prick that can play.
Tommy Dorsey

Olivia Newton-John is as antiseptic as an intensive care unit in a maternity hospital.
Clive James

Robert Plant used to send women wild with that lion's mane hairdo and half a mile of hosepipe down the front of his loons. But now everyone in music is a doe-eyed pretty boy with a Ken and Barbie andryogyno-crotch, and nothing up his nose but moisturiser.
Jeremy Clarkson

Daniel O'Donnell wouldn't say shit if his mouth was full of it.
Conor Tiernan

Paul McCartney has become the oldest living cute boy in the world.
Anne Quindlen

The triumph of Tom Jones in singles like 'It's Not Unusual' and 'Delilah' have earned him a permanent niche in the annals of nursing-home rock.
John Swenson

There are few personalities in pop music. They're mostly drab, soppy little bank clerks who've had a result.
Ian Dury

If you wind up with a boring, miserable life because you listened to your mom, your dad, your teacher, your priest, or some guy on television telling you how to do your shit, then you deserve it.
Frank Zappa

Marie Osmond is so pure, Moses couldn't even part her knees.
Joan Rivers

If white bread could sing, it would sound like Olivia Newton-John.
Geoff Dignam

I knew Doris Day before she was a virgin.
Oscar Levant

My biggest regret in life is that I didn't hit John Denver in the mouth while I had the chance.
Denis Leary

Dolly Parton reminds me of two big ice-cream cones and a whole lot of cotton candy.
Peter Allen

When I sing, everything's coming up roses. When Janis Joplin sings it's a primal scream.
Ethel Merman

Did you hear about the fellow who went into the Virgin Megastore in Dublin and bought a packet of condoms? He was too embarrassed to ask for a Daniel O'Donnell record.
K.S. Daly

Half a pint of semi-skinned milk.
Tony Parsons on Kylie Minogue

I don't think of Cliff Richard as celibate. Celibacy to me is giving up something you like, i.e. sex, and I don't think Cliff ever wanted sex in the first place - with a man *or* woman.
Bruce Welch

At worst soporific. At best, pleasantly soporific.
The New Musical Express on The Temptations

The musical equivalent of *blancmange*.
Bernard Levin on the British composer Frederick Delius

Bruce Springsteen is as useful a social commentator as Donald Duck. He's the Walt Disney of street poets.
Chris Rea

Five bowls of music looking for a spoon.
The New Musical Express on 'Yes'

Two or three catchpenny phrases served up with plenty of orchestral sugar.
George Bernard Shaw on Edward Grieg

How can they tell?
Mary Wickes after hearing Bing Crosby had died

I don't go round the place breaking up furniture. I don't spit at my public. I don't rave around the place like a lunatic 12-year-old. That gets up the noses of people who think they're radical.
Cliff Richard

The only real talent Doris Day possesses is that of being absolutely sanitary. Her personality is untouched by human emotions, her brow unclouded by human thought, her form unsmudged by the slightest form of femininity.
John Simon

All eyes, slob and slop. He couldn't open his yap without referring to his tender years. He had teeth like so many well-kept tombstones.
Julie Birchill on Donny Osmond

Working with Julie Andrews is like being hit over the head with a Valentine's card.
Christopher Plummer

Liberace is like being forcibly fed warm peppermint creams.
Clive James

Tom Jones gets underpants and hotel keys thrown at him. I get Snoopy Dolls.
Barry Manilow

If you put Ronan Keating on 'CD UK' now, I could tell you exactly what he's going to say: 'God bless you, thank you very much, love everybody.' No one learns anything. No one feels anything.
Simon Cowell

Billy Idol is the Perry Como of rock.
Johnny Rotten

Self-Portrait

I'm a window cleaner. I'm more a motherfucking window cleaner than some motherfucking motherfuckers.
Van Morrison

I don't know anything about music. In my line you don't have to.
Elvis Presley

Barry Manilow is recovering from an infection after dental surgery. When asked about it, Manilow said, 'The worst part was sitting in the dentist's chair and having to listen to my crappy music.'
Conan O'Brien

My first record was a criminal one.
Katherine Lynch

I don't normally sing, and when I sing I don't sing normally.
Danny Cummins

I have yet to record an album. I do have photo albums but I rarely listen to them these days. Who has the time?
Karl Spain

People call me the female Elvis Presley but I see myself more as a crow.
K.D. Lang

You have to be a bastard to make it in music, and the Beatles are the biggest bastards on earth.
John Lennon

I'm bigger and more dangerous than Satan.
Marilyn Manson

There's a terrible rumour going round that I only know three chords. It's a total misrepresentation of me. I actually know four.
Christy Moore

I'm a smokescreen expert. I lie all the time. It's the price of fame.
Paul McCartney

I'm so vain that when I open the fridge and the light comes on, I do twenty minutes.
Dean Martin

I sing only to punish my children.
David Feherty

I don't want to have a son because he might be like me.
Simon Cowell

Myself and Liam are lads. We've burgled houses and nicked car stereos. We like girls and swear and go to football matches and take the piss.
Noel Gallagher

I'm just a song 'n' dance man.
Bob Dylan

I don't have a drinking problem. I have a problem *not* drinking.
Dean Martin

I don't trust a single human being.
Morrissey

I'm happy to be unhappy.
Bono

I was once asked to join the Bournemouth Symphony orchestra…by the Glasgow Symphony Orchestra.
Jasper Carrott

I do not mind what language an opera is in so long as it's one I don't understand.
Sir Edward Appleton

I can't listen to that much Wagner. I start getting the urge to conquer Poland.
Woody Allen

Frankly, what I've learned in my life could be crammed in the end of a condom and shoved up a cat's arse.
David Bowie

The benefit of being a black Irishman is that I pull more chicks.
Phil Lynott

The great thing about rock 'n' roll is that a fairy like me can be a star.
Elton John

I always believed music was more important than sex. Then I thought, if I don't go to a concert for a year and a half it doesn't bother me.
Jackie Mason

I'm a concert pianist. That's a pretentious way of telling people I'm unemployed.
Oscar Levant

I don't like composers who think. It gets in the way of their plagiarism.
Howard Dietz

I like Wagner's music better than anybody's. It's so loud that one can talk the whole time without other people hearing what one says.
Oscar Wilde

I subscribe to the Evelyn Waugh school of fatherhood. The chap buggers off to Abyssinia and then sends a telegram saying, 'Have you had the child yet, and what have you called it?'
Bob Geldof

I was the pink sheep of the family.
Boy George

I don't consider myself a pessimist. I think of a pessimist as someone who's waiting for it to rain. And I feel soaked to the skin.
Leonard Cohen

I have a very finely-tuned bullshit detector.
Sharleen Spiteri

You only live once. But the way I live, that's enough.
Frank Sinatra

The three passions of my life are music, soccer and women. In that order.
Rod Stewart

I think of myself as an intelligent, sensitive human with the soul of a clown, which always forces me to blow it at the most important moments.
Jim Morrison

I'm not sure whether I'm a staggeringly extroverted latent introvert or an irritatingly introverted latent extrovert.
Sandie Shaw

I am the God of fucking.
Marilyn Manson

I'm dumb, I'm white, I'm ugly, I smell, I have freckles, I'm short, I wanna kill myself, my nose is crooked, my penis is small, I'm fucked.
Eminem

I could serve coffee using my rear as a ledge.
Jennifer Lopez

There's something about me that makes a lot of people want to throw up.
Pat Boone

My luck is so bad, if Dolly Parton had triplets, I'd be the one on the bottle.
Mel Brooks

I'll flirt with anyone, from the garbage man to grandmothers.
Madonna

Most of my lyrics are just bad mother-in-law jokes.
Billy Mackenzie

Long Time Gone

Brahms is just like Tennyson: an extraordinary musician with the brains of a third-rate village policeman.
George Bernard Shaw

If anyone has conducted a Beethoven performance and then doesn't have to go to an osteopath, there's something wrong.
Simon Rattle

Tchaikovsky's First Piano Concerto, like the first pancake, is a flop.
Nicolai Soloviev

How wonderful opera would be if there were no singers.
Gioacchino Rossini

Splitting the convulsively inflated larynx of the Muse, Alban Berg utters tortured mistuned cackling, a pandemonium of chopped-up orchestral sounds, mishandled men's throats, bestial outcries, bellowing, rattling and other evil noises. He is the poisoner of the well of German music.
Germania

I have been told that Wagner's music is better than it sounds.
Mark Twain

Classical music is the kind we keep hoping will turn into a tune.
Kin Hubbard

Too many pieces of music finish too long after the end.
Igor Stravinsky

Debussy played the piano with the lid down.
Robert Bresson

The music of Wagner imposes mental tortures that only algebra has a right to inflict.
Paul de Saint-Victor

Rossini would have been a great composer if his teacher had spanked him enough on the backside.
Ludwig von Beethoven

I have played over the music of that scoundrel Brahms. What a giftless bastard.
Pyotr Ilich Tchaikovsky

Wagner is the Puccini of music.
J.B. Morton

Most Likely You Go
Your Way (and I'll Go Mine)

The break-up of my marriage was traumatic. She wanted half of all my Billy Joel records.
Jim Rydell

When people say 'The band split due to musical differences' it means they all hated each other.
Clive Whichelow

The day I heard Michael Jackson was moving to France my sympathies, for once, were with the French.
Boy George

Courtney Love told me she'd like to sleep with me but couldn't because of the pop star thing. I said I couldn't sleep with her because of the ugly thing.
Robbie Williams

In the legal proceedings surrounding the Osmonds' split-up, Donny has been awarded custody of the teeth.
Not the Nine O'Clock News

God and I have a great relationship but we both see other people.
Dolly Parton

Filming with Barbra Streisand is an experience which may have cured me of movies.
Kris Kristofferson

A lot of break-up songs have the same theme. The guy sings, 'Baby, you're seeing somebody new now but I'll always be there for you.' They should make them more realistic: 'You're seeing someone new now, and if he beats you up – good!
Adam Sandler

Working with Cher was like being in a blender with an alligator.
Peter Bogdanovich

I believe they're giving Justin Timberlake a Lifetime Achievement Award. They're hoping he'll retire early.
Bill Dardis

We don't have a problem. I don't think about her and I don't care about her. I don't deal with the devil.
Lil Kim on fellow rapper Foxy Brown

I've spent my life running towards women and running away from them. I'd get one that looked good, had all the bodily shapes, have great sex with her and then find out that she picks

her nose. Then I was gone.
Rod Stewart

I'm not a Julie Andrews fan. I'm a diabetic.
David Janssen

I gave up movies because I got tired singing to turtles.
Elvis Presley

I went out for coffee and some newspapers and didn't come back.
John Lennon on one of his splits from Yoko Ono

I have a great many ardent fans in Ireland. There are also a good many who think I should fuck off and go live elsewhere.
Mary Coughlan

If there's anyone here I haven't insulted. I beg his pardon.
Johannes Brahms to his friends after an evening out

Every interviewer asks me the same first and second questions. Is it okay if I go to sleep?
Van Morrison

I don't like Bob Dylan's attitude. Being cheeky with the press is bad. He says he's not a singer. So why does he sing?
Tom Jones

I just made love to 25,000 people and I'm goin' home alone.
Janis Joplin after a concert in Harvard Stadium in 1970

As far as I'm concerned, Yoko was welcome to John Lennon. A dank and dreary man, he had all the sex appeal of old socks.
Joanna Trollope

I turned off Elvis when he got fat.
Cliff Richard

The groupies that followed us around in our heyday weren't so much interested in sleeping with us as reading our poetry.
Paul Simon

I never make a clean split with women. I'm a bit lily-livered for that. I just wait until I'm found out, which always happens in the end.
Rod Stewart

If a girl makes the first move, I'm off.
Cliff Richard

Like a Rolling Stone

The last Rolling Stones tour grossed more than the Gross National Product of Guyana - and had a worse human rights record.
Alexei Sayle

Keith Richards is like a monkey with arthritis.
Elton John

The word Bob Dylan used most often when he was talking about 'Like a Rolling Stone' was 'vomit.'
Howard Sounes

I've never understood what Mick Jagger saw in that buck-toothed Texas nag Jerry Hall. There are a thousand home-grown drag queens who could do her better than she does herself.
Camille Paglia

Someone has got to tell the Rolling Stones that they're no longer sexually attractive men. They look like cigarette butts with bad hair.
David Baddiel

It really bothers me that a twerp like Mick Jagger can parade around and convince everybody he's Satan. The whole thing is manipulation. He's stoned on himself.
Ry Cooder

These days it's more socially acceptable to be a pothead than a pisshead. Back in the 1960s and 1970s while half the country drove home from the pub paralytic, Mick Jagger and Keith Richards of the Rolling Stones were locked up for smoking cannabis. Now he's Sir Mick Jagger, if you don't mind.
George Best

Take a good look at Keith Richards' face. He's turned into leather. He's a giant suitcase: He has a handle on his head. That's how they move him round at concerts.
Denis Leary

Mick Jagger's great talent has always been artifice, inflation and swagger. He gradually developed his by now well-known pneumatic personality, a flexible and cartoon-like envelope that eventually became his all-purpose self.
Marianne Faithfull

I couldn't warm to Chuck Berry even if I was cremated next to him.
Keith Richards

I watched the Rolling Stones in the sixties thinking: I can sing as well as that geezer with the big lips.
Rod Stewart

Mick Jagger is about as sexy as a pissing toad.
Truman Capote

If the Stones lyrics made sense, they wouldn't be any good.
Truman Capote

From when I first met him, I saw Mick was in love with Keith. It's still that way.
Anita Pallenberg

These days Mick Jagger is more like Limping Hack Flash than Jumping Jack Flash. The band is little more than a machine for selling T-shirts.
Julie Birchill

Adolf Hitler was one of the first rock stars. Look at the way he moved. He was easily as good as Mick Jagger. He staged a country.
David Bowie

A lot of my friends have died in car crashes, plane crashes and from drug overdoses. I've learned from that. I've always made sure I avoided driving while on a drug overdose during a plane flight.
Mick Jagger

It's no fun being at loggerheads with me. I can drain the energy out of anyone that fights with me. I don't enjoy it but I can be a hard fucker.
Keith Richards

Mick is a lovely bunch of guys.
Richards on Jagger

My mother has always been unhappy with me being a rock star. She'd much rather I did something nicer, like being a bricklayer.
Mick Jagger

Mick Jagger's lips are so big he could frenchkiss a moose.
Joan Rivers

If I ever met Keith Richards again I'd say, 'Listen, I don't want to talk to you. I want to interview your liver.'
Nick Kent

It Hurts Me Too

According to *Time* magazine, Christina Aguilera's music is being used down in Guantanamo Bay to torture prisoners.
Jay Leno

I loved Amy Winehouse but sometimes she sounded like a duck trying to shit.
Jonathan Ross

How do you make a cello sound beautiful? Sell it and buy a violin.
Bruno Kassel

Commenting on the Eurovision Song contest sometimes makes you lose the will to live.
Marty Whelan

Sleep is an excellent way of listening to an opera.
James Stephens

Nothing soothes me more after a long and maddening course of pianoforte recitals than to sit and have my teeth drilled.
George Bernard Shaw

I would rather eat my testicles than re-form The Smiths. And that's saying something for a vegetarian.
Morrissey

Oscar & Hammerstein's *Flower Drum Song* is so bad, at times I longed for the boy-meets-tractor theme of Soviet drama.
Bernard Levin

I take music pretty seriously. You see that scar on my wrist? I heard the Bee Gees were getting back together.
Denis Leary

There are some things that just aren't done, such as drinking Dom Perignon '53 at a temperature of 38 degrees Fahrenheit. Or listening to the Beatles without earmuffs.
Ian Fleming

Humphrey Searle writes music that sounds like the theme from *Star Wars* played backwards through a washing machine.
Clive James

I went to see Pavarotti once. He doesn't like it when you join in.
Mick Miller

If you eat a lot of Indian food it can damage your taste. I was in India last year, for instance, and I found myself listening to Michael Bolton.
Jimmy Carr

What's the difference between a drummer and a vacuum cleaner? You have to plug in a vacuum cleaner before it sucks.
Don Rickles

If you can imagine a man having a vasectomy without an anaesthetic to the sound of frantic sitar-playing, you will have some idea what popular Turkish music is like.
Bill Bryson

My wife takes me to the opera so often I've now learned to snore in Italian.
Henny Youngman

David Lee Roth sounds like Tom Waits after a tracheotomy.
Ken Tucker

I feel like Bob Dylan has been sleeping in my mouth.
Elvis Presley after a bad day in the recording studio

Michael Bolton sounds as if he's having his teeth drilled by Helen Keller.
Jeff Wilder

A friend of mine wanted to be a pop star but he had to give it up when they found out he could sing.
Lambert Jeffries

Would he have said it best if he said nothing at all?
Joe Duffy on Ronan Keating's autobiography

The trouble with a folk song is that once you've played it through there's nothing much you can do except play it again – louder.
Constance Lambert

I sometimes wonder which would be nicer, an opera without an interval or an interval without an opera.
Ernest Newman

The more people piss me off, the more I have to write about.
Eminem

Daniel O'Donnell once worked as a dishwasher. He didn't last long because he loved to sing while he worked.
Dave O'Connell

The English may not like music but they absolutely love the sound it makes.
Sir Thomas Beecham

I spent many years laughing at Harry Secombe's singing until somebody told me it wasn't a joke.
Spike Milligan

Live music is an anachronism. Now is the winter of our discotheque.
Benny Green

An incurable music lover is someone who'll buy a set of drums for their id.
Terry Martin

After playing Chopin I feel as if I'd been weeping over sins never committed.
Oscar Wilde

To me a night at the opera means watching a play I don't like, sung in a language I don't understand, wearing a tuxedo that doesn't fit.
Gene Perret

My ultimate vocation in life is to be an irritant.
Elvis Costello

A film musician is like a mortician. He can't bring the body back to life but he's still expected to make it look better.
Adolph Deutsch

Movie music is noise. It's even more painful than my sciatica.
Sir Thomas Beecham

Just Like a Woman

She really was a bad-looking girl. Facially she resembled Louis Armstrong's voice.
Woody Allen

Mariah Carey was a huge booking for *So Graham Norton*. If Jesus himself had agreed to do the show, I doubt his PR would have made such a fuss.
Graham Norton

While a girl is waiting for the right man to come along, she can have some pretty good fun with a wrong ones.
Cher

Women should be obscene and not heard.
John Lennon

I smoke weed and I masturbate. I don't do both at the same time. That gets tricky.
Sinead O'Connor

I'm a size queen. If I'm on a date and I see the guy isn't packing, that's when I fake a backache.
Janet Jackson

There is no female Mozart for the same reason that there's no female Jack the Ripper.
Camille Paglia

When she started to play, Steinway came down personally and rubbed his name off the piano.
Bob Hope

If a horse could sing in a monotone it would sound like Carly Simon, except a horse wouldn't try to rhyme 'yacht' with 'apricot' and 'gavotte'.
Robert Christgau

Madam, I have cried only twice in my life. Once when I dropped a wing of truffled chicken into Lake Como. The other time was when I heard you sing.
Gioacchino Rossini

She's a singer we put to the back… of the car park.
Alan Ayckbourn

Barbra Streisand has all the talent of a butterfly's fart.
Walter Matthau

Tina Turner is all legs and hair, with a mouth that could swallow a whole football stadium – including the hot dog stand.
Laura Lee Davies

She Tarzan, he Jane.
Andrew Morton on Posh Spice and David Beckham

When she was going through her virginal, Barbie-doll phase, Britney Spears was like any other insipid popstar: ultra-serious and devoid of personality. She's got a lot more likeable since going off the rails. She parties in public now, she looks dishevelled, and she's got acne.
Mary Carr

Desolation Row

When Don Baker sings, out comes the desolation of a million empty railway stations.
Pat Ingoldsby

My best songs come from suffering because I've indulged my masochism.
Annie Lennox

You know it's a bad day when you wake up and the birds are singing Leonard Cohen numbers.
Jenny Eclair

I would never do anything as vulgar as having fun.
Morrissey

I stopped believing in Santa Claus the day my mother brought me to the mall as a child and he asked me for my autograph.
Judy Garland

Hate makes the world go round.
Morrissey

The worst day in the history of rock 'n' roll music was the day Donny Osmond was born.
Mick Jagger

After the Beatles broke up I thought my life was over. A barrelling empty feeling just rolled across my soul. I remember days when I woke up at three in the afternoon and thought 'There's no point in getting up, it'll soon be bedtime'.
Paul McCartney

Being a rock star is the most boring, short term, depressing thing you can be. I'd rather grow a pot plant of tomatoes.
Chris Rea

Of all modern phenomena, the most monstrous and ominous, the most manifestly rotting with disease, the most grimly prophetic of destruction, the most clearly and unmistakeably inspired by evil spirits, the most instantly and awfully overshadowed by the wrath of heaven, the most near to madness and moral chaos, the most vivid with devilry and despair, is the practice of having to listen to loud music while eating a meal in a restaurant.
G.K. Chesterton

There's a lot of places in the world that suck but I'll keep that shit confidential. People might buy my records there.
Eminem

At the end of the world, the two things that will be left are cockroaches and Cher.
J. Randy Tarraborelli